SOVEREIGNTY
GRACE & GLORY

SOVEREIGNTY
GRACE & GLORY

**The Beauty of God's Character
and Plan for the World**

BOB LENZ

ARPress
ILLUMINATING IDEAS
EMPOWERING VOICES

ARPress
45 Dan Road Suite 5
Canton MA 02021
Hotline: 1(888) 821-0229
Fax: 1(508) 545-7580

Ordering Information:
Quantity sales. Special discounts are available on quantity purchases by corporations, associations, and others. For details, contact the publisher at the address above.

Printed in the United States of America.

ISBN-13:	Softcover	979-8-89330-693-4
	eBook	979-8-89330-692-7
	Hardback	979-8-89330-950-8

Library of Congress Control Number: 2024902480

Table of Contents

DEDICATION

This book is affectionately dedicated to the multitude of college and seminary students, small groups, Sunday School and Bible study men and women I have taught over the years. My students, especially those overseas at the Erikson-Tritt Bible College in Papua, Indonesia, have challenged me to dig into the Word of God, and helped me to grow in the knowledge of His Word and of the Lord. They have helped me to formulate a theology which is God centered. I am the richer for every person God has brought into my life in these classes.

I am also indebted to those who helped me prepare this volume, especially to my wife Shirley, and to Greg Hazard, who have read the manuscript and contributed helpful suggestions and corrections to the book.

ENDORSEMENTS

"This book ties together the great themes of the sovereignty of God, the grace of God and the glory of God in a way that puts the emphasis on missions. The last chapter where Bob ties together all of these themes and shows how they motivate missions is worth the price of the book! With the discussion questions in the back, this would make a great small group study, especially for those who want a solid theological grounding for the work of world missions."

Tom Siefert—Pastor Mona Shores Baptist Church
Muskegon, MI

Good mission practices and good missiology must be built on...solid theology. This book does that in a fresh and thoughtful way. Lenz skillfully weaves together the interrelated themes of God's sovereignty, grace, and glory to lead the reader to a greater understanding of God's mission in the world. This update on three core theological themes brings in turn, a clearer understanding of how and why we should engage the world in mission.

Marvin Newell—Senior Vice President Missio Nexus

In Sovereignty, Grace and Glory, Bob Lenz has turned a biblical eye on the three dynamic realities that condition Christian growth and experience. Bob and his wife Shirley have a background of missionary experience in Irian Jaya, Indonesia and active mission mobilization in North America. They have experienced what Bob is talking about, through good times and struggles. I have known and fellowshipped with Bob through many years. If we can comprehend the depth of meaning behind the fact that God is in control - his sovereignty, that he deals with us in constant grace, and sets before us a great and eternal destiny-glory, we'll be able to persevere and thrive joyfully, no matter what happens to us. Bob Lenz understands and communicates this. You'll be blessed and helped by reading it.

Mike Pocock, D.Miss
Senior Professor and Chairman Emeritus
World Missions and Intercultural Studies
Dallas Theological Seminary

Christian life is most enjoyable if one realizes in his/her head of God's sovereignty, he/she will find peace in his/her heart that is based on the assurance of God's grace, therefore will be ready to strive to honor God with glory that is due him. Readers of this volume will enjoy the labor of the author who has skillfully tackled deep concepts (e.g. the sovereignty of God), unpacked complicated passages (e.g. the prologue of the Epistle to the Ephesians), and illustrated abstract ideas (e.g. the magnificence of God). The result is a light reading on heavy ideas in Christian faith but a helpful guide in Christian living: informative and inspiring.

This book can also be used in a group setting, even at high school level, by using "questions for discussion" of each chapter. It is my pleasure to recommend this book for leisurely reading and can be a good gift to new converts. The table below shows how the three themes being weaved together in this book are closely related to the theological understanding of the nature of God and the created order.

Theme	God's Nature	Created Order
sovereignty	transcendental	above space & time
grace	providential	able to bless
glory	teleological	able to bring all things to honor Himself

Enoch Wan,
Former President of Evangelical Missiological Society (2008-2014)

INTRODUCTION

Sovereignty - The Mystery of God
Grace - The Method of God
Glory - The Magnificence of God

There is always a danger in over simplifying the Christian life with phrases such as "Seven Steps to…" or "Five Secrets of…." No one wants to make the Christian life a mechanical exercise of doing something. I want to avoid that pitfall as well. Nevertheless, as I have studied Scripture for a number of years, three themes continue to surface. These three concepts have an integral relationship that I believe God desires the believer to assimilate into the fabric of his Christian life. The concepts are summarized with the three words which I have used as the title of the book. If you get hold of the principles behind these words, you will not only live a spiritually satisfying life, but also will live the life that God designed for you. And when He designs something, it must be for your good and happiness. Briefly stated: God is in sovereign control of our lives. We may not understand all of the mysteries that surround our lives, or the whys and wherefores of our circumstances. We are forever asking why did God allow this or that.

Everyone that has been born or that will be born has come into this world under His careful eye and planning. Everything that we are or have is from Him, and He designed it from eternity. In addition to orchestrating our lives, God has given us the wherewithal to live the life that He has designed. He has provided us with His grace both for salvation and for daily living. We need to make a distinction between mercy and grace, and we will do that later. But for now, in summary, we have no resources in ourselves that will bring us to the end result that God designs for us. If God does not provide us with His daily grace, we will fail miserably. We may think that we are clever or resourceful to live our lives apart from His help, but we are fooling ourselves.

But we also ask ourselves: "Why has God brought us into this world, and allowed us to live as we do? What is the purpose of our lives?" The answer is to please and honor Him. The catechism of the Reformed Church asks the question: "what is the chief end of man?" The student responds with the answer: "to glorify God and enjoy Him forever." The sole purpose of our lives is for God's glory and "eternal satisfaction." Just stop and think of that truth. God does everything possible and imaginable to help us fulfill what He has designed us for by taking control of, providing for, and helping us end with a life that not only brings us enjoyment, but brings him satisfaction.

As I pondered this truth, it struck me forcefully that this is also God's plan to bring a lost world to Himself. In fact, the careful study that we will pursue in this book will show that from the beginning of humankind, God wants to carry out that plan in the lives of every person on earth. Unfortunately, sin has marred this beautiful plan, and humanity has gone its own way, thinks that they can make it on their own, and lives for their own glory and selfish purposes. Even professing believers live confused lives because they fail to see this design from their Lord and Savior. But God cares enough for His creation that He has worked a beautiful pattern which not only includes those who have heard the Gospel and have had the opportunity to respond to it, but also those who have never heard those truths that God has beautifully woven for His non-believing creation.

At first blush, you might think that this is some great theological treatise or complicated scheme that only a few can understand. As I study this subject, I am amazed to see how simple these truths are, that even a young person can comprehend the mystery of this plan. God knows that we are finite and cannot comprehend His infinite mind. So He has purposefully made it simple enough for us to grasp in order to respond to Him in the way He designed for us to live. After all, when we think of the widespread cultures of humankind throughout the world, there are many who have a lack of understanding God. They have never even heard of His name. Therefore the Lord has to place it on a level that all people can grasp so as to fulfill His plan and purpose for their lives when it is explained to them.

This Biblical plan is foundational in witnessing and evangelism. How often has a Christian used the statement in sharing the Gospel: "God has a wonderful plan for your life."? What he is saying basically is that God is sovereign in lives, has laid out something beautiful for humanity, and wants to intercept a wasted life by restoring it to the original purpose that He created for that person to live. The witness then goes on to say that humankind cannot do anything to obtain salvation except by grace through faith in the work of Christ, and when believers do come to faith in Christ, they cannot live the Christian life apart from the grace that God provides for them (Eph. 2:8-10). Finally, he might add that those who follow Christ must surrender their lives to the Lord (Rom. 12:1-2) and not live for themselves. In so doing, believers honor God with their lives. That is another way of saying that believers desire to bring glory to God. Ephesians 2:10 conveys a similar truth because God wants us to do the things that He has planned for us to accomplish in order that we may attain maximum benefit and joy while at the same time bring maximum honor and glory to Him. That accomplishment can only be obtained by God's grace actively at work in us.

The goal of the book is to make this user friendly to the lay person even though there are some technical and theological terms included. The book will have a solid Biblical base and can be incorporated into small group Bible studies, personal evangelism courses, or as a personal guide in witnessing. My greater vision is that this study will prompt people to consider a lost world that needs the Savior, and so touch lives that people will believe that they can be witnesses, not only in their homeland, but where the name of Jesus has never been heard. The seminal thoughts for this book will be taken from Ephesians 1:3-14, that great one sentence passage (in the original) that Paul wrote under inspiration when he communicated the letter to the Ephesian Church. That epistle deals with the person of Jesus Christ and His headship over the Church. But Paul goes back in time to reveal the original plan of God which included the salvation of the elect and the incorporation of these believers into the family of God, His Church. We will examine his logical layout of this truth under the aspects of sovereignty, grace and glory.

All Biblical quotes are taken from the New King James version unless otherwise indicated.

PART ONE – THE SOVEREIGNTY OF GOD

CHAPTER 1
SOVEREIGNTY - THE MYSTERY OF GOD IN ALL THINGS

We have to start with a disclaimer: we will never fully understand the mystery of God. Having said that, we must not shy away from attempting to delve into the mystery of His heart simply because we are finite and He is infinite. He has left us enough information in His inspirited Word for us to understand in general the ways that He works, without fully comprehending all of the mysteries of His character. To understand the concept of sovereignty to the extent that we can is to grasp the foundation of our faith. That is why Paul begins the Ephesian letter the way he does. He begins with God's mysterious foreordained plan, and proceeds to develop the truth of salvation by grace, and the resultant glory He receives from His great plan of redemption both in the individual and in the Church, which is composed of redeemed individuals.

Let's begin with a simple definition of the word sovereignty. It is the supremacy of God to do anything He wants to do in heaven and earth without the interference of man or angelic being to hinder those actions. He is all powerful and nothing can hinder His purposes or oppose His will. The wise reader of scripture will immediately raise a red flag and say "But what about the passages in the Bible that talk of man choosing, or in popular parlance, man has free will?" If God is sovereign and man freely rebels against Him, is that an act of God, or a decree that He has set forth in which man has no choice but to do that sinful thing? Does that make God the author of sin? These are valid questions not to be taken lightly. The simple, but profound answer is that God is sovereign over everything without being culpable or guilty of evil or wrong doing. This is the mystery of all things. How can God make sovereign decisions that seem to implicate Him in evil (at least from man's viewpoint)? To understand this is to become like Him, infinite in knowledge and wisdom. We can never fathom the depths of His wisdom to rule the world justly and righteously despite all of the wickedness that occurs in it. We must leave that mystery wrapped up in His righteous and loving heart, and trust Him to be who He says that He is in the Bible; God most holy and without sin.

In the book *For the Fame of God's Name: Essays in Honor of John Piper,* Bruce Ware gives this definition of sovereignty which seems to be all encompassing of God's purposes, ***God exhaustively plans and meticulously carries out His perfect will as He alone knows is best, regarding all that is in heaven and on earth, and He does so without failure or defeat, accomplishing His purposes in all of creation from the smallest details to the grandest purposes of His plan for the whole of the created order. (Piper 2010, 128).***

This quotation from Ware succinctly summarizes how God acts toward His creation from His own viewpoint. But we must also make a distinction between the thought of a sovereign God working His plan, and the terms *fatalism* or *determinism*. Fatalism as defined by Peter Thussen is "The absolute and unalterable determination of all things by an impersonal force" (Thussen 2009, 5). Determinism implies that certain causes determine certain outcomes, whether those causes are God related or man related.

The word sovereignty when used in connection with the person and plan of God, is more of a theological word. In the Old Testament, the word that is translated sovereign in the New International Version (NIV) frequently refers to the Hebrew name of God which is, *Adonai*, meaning Lord. In the New Testament, there are words that are used or translated in conjunction with the sovereignty of God, such as predestined, foreknowledge, foreseeing, and chosen. We will define these words below to convey what is meant when we talk about God's sovereignty.

Another facet in defining the sovereignty of God is to say that God is all in all, and everything has its beginning and ending in Him. 1 Chronicles 29:11 says, "Yours O LORD, is the greatness, the power, and the glory, the victory, and the majesty: for all that is in the heaven and in earth is Yours; Yours is the kingdom, O LORD, and You are exalted as Head above all."

That verse just about sums up who God is. His supremacy is seen in everything He is, does, and allows (cf. Ps. 89:11; 1 Tim. 6:15). He sets up kings and brings them down (Ps. 75:6-7). He exercises His right to do anything He wants anytime He chooses with all of His creatures.

This will include miraculous acts that defy or go against the normal laws of nature, such as Jesus feeding 5000 with five loaves and two fish. There are also what we would call His superintending acts i.e. actions that do not go against nature, but are under His sovereign watch care to change the events of the situation, such as the release of Peter from prison (Acts Ch. 12), or, on a practical level, protecting a house in the midst of a tornado. We think of those kinds of deliverances as miraculous because they would not have happened had God not intervened. But no law of nature was "broken" to accomplish His will in the act. God redirected the sequence of happenings to appear to be miraculous, and we give Him the glory and credit for the deliverance just as we would give Him in performing miraculous acts. The multitude of events in our lives that we think of as miraculous are not really that, but rather the superintending intervention of God to change the course of that event. Just think of the times that drivers have been spared from seeming accidents, avoiding injury or death. God displays His sovereignty to act on our behalf in those events. He is able to do that because of His character and attributes which include His omnipotence, omniscience, omnipresence, eternality, infiniteness, grace, mercy, love, and a host of other attributes which are in perfection.

In Ephesians 1:5, Paul states that God "Predestined us to adoption as sons by Jesus Christ." In Ephesians 1:11 we are "Predestined according to the purpose of Him Who works all things after the counsel of His will." The word predestined is *proorizo*. The word basically means to predetermine, foreordain, to decide or appoint beforehand. Hendriksen translates that word "pre-encircled" (Hendriksen 1967, 5). That is very descriptive, as it pictures God's chosen people as being completely encompassed by the sovereignty of God.

The New Testament usage generally refers to God's decision making or His decree from eternity. The word is used in six places in the New Testament; Acts 4:28; Rom. 8:29, 30; Eph. 1:5, 11, and 1 Cor. 2:7. In two of the passages (Acts 4:28; 1 Cor. 2:7), the word is used in connection with God orchestrating prior events. In the other four passages, the word is used in connection with God's prior relationship to people. In the better known Rom. 8:29 passage Paul says, "Whom He foreknew He also predestined." 1 Cor. 2:7 tells of the wisdom that "God ordained before the ages for our glory." The Acts passage refers to the prayer of believers recognizing the hand of God in the death of Christ. He predestined the Savior's death, and allowed man to carry out that plan under His sovereign control.

In all six instances of the usage of the word predestine, God is the one who pre-determines the events of mankind. Not only that, but in every instance, the word is used in the aorist tense. Many grammarians have defined the aorist tense in various ways, but a succinct meaning would be that it is an action completed in the past without making mention of a time or progress as to its accomplishments or completeness. It is a simple occurrence of an act. God in His sovereignty at some point in past time determined the destiny of all things, especially in the setting apart of people for salvation. God gives no reason for His action, or who and how He determined should be included in this action. He simply states that this is what He did without being influenced or motivated by anything outside of Himself. Here is where the mystery of His sovereignty enters the picture. Knowing the nature of God Who is only goodness and righteousness (plus a whole host of other glorious perfect characteristics), He has designed a salvation that is perfect in its execution for all mankind as only a perfect God could administer. We must conclude that a sovereign God creates all things with a perfect ending, or He cannot be the God of the Bible.

Not only that, God cannot be influenced, bribed, or coerced to do anything based on what man might desire Him to do. As John Piper states "God is not constrained by anything outside of Himself to do anything He does not want to do" (Piper 1987, 2). Certainly no one can bribe Him since He is the Creator of all things, and does not need anything from man to satisfy or please Him. In the same way, He cannot be influenced by anything that man can offer to make Him happy, or to do anything for Him, since His happiness and satisfaction are secure within Himself. Psalm 135:6 says "Whatever the Lord pleases, He does in heaven and in earth." This is another way of saying that He is sovereign and determines all things beforehand.

Another word used in conjunction with the sovereignty of God is the Greek word *proginosko*, which basically means to know beforehand. We get the English words "prognosis" and prognosticate" from the root word. The Jews knew of Paul's life (or beforehand) Acts: 26:5. Peter refers to the diaspora who knew certain facts beforehand about the scriptures (2 Pet. 3:17). It is also used of God's knowing beforehand in Rom. 8:29 and 1 Pet. 1:20. In the Romans' passage, God foreknew those who were called for salvation and so were foreordained (*proorizo*). In the Peter passage, Jesus Christ was foreknown before the foundation of the world. The King James version translates the word "foreordained", while the NIV uses the word "chosen". But it is the word *proginosko*. The noun form of this word is used by Peter in His Pentecost sermon in Acts 2:23 with regard to the death of Christ. The word translated there is foreknowledge. The Romans passage is in the aorist tense, and the Peter passage is in the past perfect tense. Again we conclude that God is working in eternity past to perform acts that only He decides should transpire.

A third word that can be connected with the sovereignty of God is the word *eklego*, or *eklegomai*, meaning to be chosen. This word is used in a wide variety of ways in scripture from choosing one thing over another (Luke 10:42), to the choosing of Jesus' disciples (John 6:70). The word itself is usually expressed in the past tense, and is especially true as used in Ephesians 1:4. Believers have been chosen in Christ before the foundation of the world. The verb is in the aorist tense and the middle voice, which refers to choosing for oneself. God sovereignly chose for Himself, according to His own standards, who would become believers. As an illustration; a person goes to the market to buy some peaches. In choosing the fruit, he will examine carefully the condition of the fruit for ripeness, and to assure that none are spoiled. He then chooses what he thinks are the best among the available choices. The fruit has nothing to say as to who chooses it. In the sovereignty of God, no "fruit" is good because all men are sinners. God chooses among the fallen sinners of mankind a people whom He in His sovereignty decides will be part of His family, apart from any goodness or favorableness of mankind. A person has nothing to say or to offer anything to God that will persuade the mind of the Lord to choose him/her. In that choosing, there is not necessarily a rejection of the one who is not chosen since God loves the entire world. It is only a choosing of what God deems to be appropriate for His own cause and pleasure.

Thussen makes a keen observation in discussing Paul's choosing of Israel in Romans chapters 9-11. Why does the apostle emphasize God's sovereignty here, as well as in the great Ephesians one passage? Thussen observes that the reason may have been the marvelous Damascus Road conversion of Paul, who was called by God for a special purpose (Thussen 2009, 19). Certainly Paul himself reiterates this in amazement, and confesses his unworthiness to be called an apostle: (see 1 Cor. 15:8-9; Gal. 1:15; 1 Tim. 1:12-16). He recognizes that God did not have to make Paul His servant. Nor did God see that the persecutor Saul would become the apostle Paul, and so ordained his salvation. Rather, God sovereignly chose the persecutor Saul in order to change him and make him to become the apostle Paul. The choice was God's not Paul's. The decision was made unconditionally; that is, Paul had no say in God's choosing Him other than to respond to His divine election and calling. This is what he emphasizes so clearly in Galatians 1:15, "*When it pleased God* (italics mine), who separated me from my mother's womb and called me by His grace." The *Theological Dictionary of the New Testament* notes that the word choose means "to take pleasure or delight in, be glad in" (Kittel Vol. 2 1965, 738). God took delight in Paul from eternity long before Paul was Saul the persecutor.

In Romans 9:15-23, a conundrum faces the student of the Word. One could take from this passage the fact that God predestines people to hell, because He says in verse 15, "I will have mercy on whomever I will have mercy, and I will have compassion on whomever I will have compassion." But a closer examination of the context may bring us to a different conclusion. In verse 22 we note that God is longsuffering. He is not willing that any should perish. The end of that verse says that they (the unbelievers) are "prepared for destruction." The verse does not say that God prepared them for destruction. It only says that they were prepared for destruction. We cannot attribute the fate of unbelievers to God. Because of their sin, the unbeliever has prepared himself for destruction, and must receive the wrath of God because of His holiness. Compare this with the next verse which says, "He (God) had prepared (believers) beforehand for glory." Notice the past tense (actually aorist tense in the Greek) for both the words prepared and called in the next verse. God prepared His elect for glory from eternity past (so Romans 8: 29-30), but the unbeliever prepared himself for destruction. That does not refer to annihilation, but to separation from God for eternity in hell.

Another way to deal with the dilemma of sovereignty and free will is to ask the question about the sinfulness of humankind in relation to God's choosing people for salvation. If, as some say, God grants grace to all men initially (a concept which does not seem to be biblical) so that all can be saved, and He then chooses some for salvation while neglecting to choose others, He is capricious and cruel since all people should be saved by that initial grace. But all people are sinners (which is stated clearly in the Bible) and have no right to claim anything from God but rather to receive condemnation and separation from Him. They are destined for hell. Now God intervenes and rescues some from this fate by giving them the ability to choose Him. He is then a merciful God. The manner in which He chooses is still a mystery, but reflects His loving character to rescue some from condemnation. From the illustration above, we can draw the general principle that God is constantly in the business of choosing people for salvation. We must never think of Him as being reluctant to want to redeem humankind because of sinfulness. Indeed, God is holy and cannot tolerate the presence of sin or sinful people. But as holy as He is, He is also loving and not willing that any should perish, but rather that they have eternal life (John 3:16). To that extent, He continually seeks humankind, even though they continually reject Him, and indeed are dead in sin so that they cannot seek God of their own accord. This makes His sovereignty more majestic in choosing reluctant, sinful and incapable people to be part of His eternal plan. John Piper makes a cogent observation, ***Death and misery of the unrepentant is in and of itself no delight to God. God is not a sadist. He is not malicious or bloodthirsty. Instead, when a rebellious, wicked, unbelieving person is judged, what God delights in is the vindication of truth and goodness and of His own honor and glory. (Piper Feb.1, 1987, 6).***

In delineating these truths, it would appear that we have a conflict or inconsistency between the method of God's choosing and the response of man in accepting the sovereign will of God. But a careful study of scripture reveals that there is no inconsistency between the two. This is part of the mystery that we will never understand, We must believe and accept both parts of this mysterious equation, while at the same time allowing God to be God in whatever he chooses to do. J.I. Packer says of this seeming dilemma, ***We shall not oppose them to each other. Nor shall we qualify, or modify, or water down, either of them in terms of the other, for this is not what the Bible does either. What the Bible does is to assert both truths side by side in the strongest and most unambiguous terms as two ultimate facts. (Packer 1961, 35).***

In our own finite way, whenever we are faced with a seeming dilemma about God's actions, we should choose as an option the "default" mode in the computer of our minds. That default mode is to give the benefit of doubt to the glory of God. Paul does this in Romans chapter 9. He answers those who wrestle with the purpose of God in electing Israel, and cannot understand God's workings in choosing Jacob over Esau (Rom. 9:13). Charles Hodge says of this, "It is not unjust for God to exercise His sovereignty in the distribution of His mercies, for He expressly claims the right" ((Hodge 1993, 284). Paul continues to answer this wrestling in verse 16 when he mentions that God raised up Pharaoh to execute His sovereign will. Again, God has the prerogative to do that. To the person who says "That is not fair" Paul summarizes with the statement in Romans 9:18-21, *Therefore He has mercy on whom He wills, and whom He Wills He hardens. You will say to me then "Why does He still find fault?" For who has resisted His will? But indeed, O man, who are you to reply against God? Will the thing formed say to him who formed it, "Why have you made me like this?" Does not the potter have power over the clay from the same lump to make one vessel for honor, and another for dishonor?*

Paul's answer to the mystery of God's working is that He is God, and we are not God. God has the lawful right to do as He chooses. Let that be the final answer for the questioning of His acts when we do not understand His ways.

The importance of these word studies is to lay a foundation that shows the mystery of God in dealing with His world, and especially with His elect. God is the source of all things created and is sovereign in the way He deals with that creation. Because He is that source, all creatures are dependent on Him for their survival. That puts God in the supreme position of having the final say as to the fate of His creation since no one can tell Him what He should do. This is especially true when it comes to our salvation. In His sovereignty, He chose a mysterious plan that only He could devise, i.e. to choose the second Person of the Trinity to become like we are in the person of His Son Jesus, and to have Jesus sacrifice Himself on the cross to pay for the sins of humankind.

In thinking about sharing the Gospel of Christ with others, we should have the under- standing of these beliefs in the arsenal of truth in our minds, but this is certainly not necessary to present to the unbeliever as we attempt to win that person to Christ. It would be ludicrous to approach a person with the intent to witness, and then remind him after he does profess Christ, that God had this in mind for that person before the foundation of the world. We do not dump the entire theology of redemption on a person when that person professes Christ as Savior. Our response to his belief is to rejoice with Him that he received Christ, as God gave him the understanding by His Spirit to believe by faith in the finished work of the Savior. As this brother or sister grows in faith and understanding, we can disciple that person and help him/her to realize that this was indeed God's eternal plan from the foundation of the world. By the same token, we would not tell a person who rejects our witness that God may have predestined that person to hell (which actually is not true) if he/she does not receive our witness and repent. To make such a statement is both unwise and judgmental. We do not know what God has in mind for anyone's future. Our responsibility is to tell the good news of the Gospel of Jesus Christ to that person and let God deal with the destiny of his/her soul.

One final thought before proceeding with this study. The foundation of these thoughts, as mentioned above, is taken from Ephesians chapter 1. The epistle itself is a study of God's work in the church, its unity, and place in the world, and not as much as looking at the individual. The theme of the book is the Church, with Christ as the Head. True, individuals make up the Church. As such, individuals will be a large part of the focus of the study. But bear in mind that Paul uses the plural when addressing the readers of this letter. He speaks to the group of believers and the relationship of these truths with respect to the manner in which they, the Church, fulfill this plan of sovereignty, grace, and glory in the world. Although we may look at the individual in relation to these truths, we must not forget that God is looking at the world through the eyes of His Church which He established. Having defined some of the words connected with God's sovereignty, let us proceed to see how the Bible reveals this truth.

CHAPTER 2
SOVEREIGNTY - PAUL'S STATEMENT IN EPHESIANS 1:3-14

One of the key words in this passage is *praise* or blessing, used three times. It is the Greek word *eulogia in noun form* or *eulogeo* in verb form. The word itself has the idea of speaking well of, or extolling. What is most interesting is that within the word *eulogeo* is the concept of the word "logos." The word *logos* could be translated as thought or word. This implies that there is a conscious thought of speaking well or extolling someone. Paul is absolutely ecstatic in his conscious praise for what God has done, which he explains in the following verses.

The apostle then states in Ephesians 1:3 the blessings that God has bestowed upon us in Christ Jesus. It is "every spiritual blessing," it is "in the heavenlies," and it is "in Christ." The use of the word or phrase containing the concept of the heavenlies is one of Paul's favorite expressions in this book, and is used in four other places (1:20; 2:6; 3:10; 6:12). What are these heavenlies? In 1:3, 1:20, and 2:6; the heavenlies refer to the place where Christ dwells. Believers who are "in Christ" are viewed by God as joined in relationship to Christ where He dwells. But Ephesians 3:10 and 6:12 make reference to principalities and powers dwelling in the heavenlies. There is a realm of the universe where a spiritual warfare is taking place between the forces of good and evil. The believer is in that heavenly realm only in the sense of a spiritual transaction (so Longman and Garland 2006, 48) where he is seated with Christ in those heavenly realms. The reality of this transaction i.e. seated with Christ in the heavenlies will happen eventually, but in God's mind it has already happened, and that is how He views the believer in Christ presently.

All that the Sovereign God has given us is "in Christ." That phrase "in Christ" is used eleven times in the book of Ephesians. Paul also uses the phrase "in Him" or "in whom" (Christ) eleven other times in the book. Nothing that we have is of any merit of our own. It is all of God, whether it is our choosing, the method by which He accomplishes this purpose, or the results of His actions. That is why Paul says in Romans 11:36, "For of Him, and through Him, and to Him are all things, to whom be glory forever, Amen." Now Paul begins to describe some of those blessings. We should note first that we often think or speak of material blessings when we think of the blessings of God on a life. In fact, the Old Testament saints believed that spiritual blessings were more important than material blessings. Think of Abraham and especially the passage in Hebrews. 11:9-10 where this rich herdsman is more interested in spiritual thoughts than in his earthly possessions. David the rich king who had everything materially than a person could desire reveled in God's promise to him of an eternal dynasty to his descendants (2 Samuel 7:18-29). Nevertheless, to some extent, Old Testament believers did seem to equate material blessings with God's favor upon their lives. But the New Testament definitely emphasizes the spiritual blessings, over the material ones

(2 Cor. 4:18) despite the fact that all material blessings as well come from a sovereign God. Note that Paul uses the word "every" in Ephesians chapter one verse three referring to spiritual blessings. He may have wanted to distinguish between the Old and New Covenants to his readers. This is where Paul is taking us in this passage when he stresses the blessings originating in the heavenlies and are connected with Christ.

In chapter one, we mentioned briefly the usage of the word *proorizo* as found in Ephesians chapter one, verses five and eleven. Paul is so carried away with all that the Trinity has done, he cannot cease to extol the magnificence of God and His plan for believers. Furthermore, he ties the three concepts of sovereignty, grace, and glory together in this passage. When we examine the concept of predestination and compare that with the passage in Romans 8:29, we note that our predestination is connected with our election and choosing. We are predestined to sonship, but chosen in sonship to be holy. God, in His sovereignty, determined before the creation of the world that we would be predestined to become His sons by faith in Jesus Christ. Another way to state this is to say that the plan of God was to predestine who would be saved, and the election of God is the manner in which He chooses individuals to fulfill His plan. Paul states in Eph. 1:4-5, "Just as He chose us in Him before the foundation of the world, that we should be holy and without blame before Him in love, having predestinated us to adoption as sons by Jesus Christ to Himself, according to the good pleasure of His will."

The sovereignty of God is seen in the very opening of this magnificent praise. It is from the foundation of the world that God has chosen His elect. Remember that Paul is speaking of the elect as the Church which is His body, even though we often look at these verses as an individual experiencing salvation. (Certainly the Church is made up of individuals). We should note in this and other passages connected with this theme, God never explains why or justifies the reason that He has chosen people from the foundation of the world. He simply does this of His own volition. He does not owe anyone an explanation of His actions. This may be a hard pill for some of us to swallow, but The Sovereign of the universe has a right to act as He chooses. The amazing thing is that He chooses to act at all in love toward His creatures, especially as He sees them from eternity's perspective as sinful beings who want nothing to do with Him. The only response He desires from us is that we fall at His feet in humble adoration for the fact of our being chosen by Him.

In verse four, the foundational blessing is that of God choosing us for Himself (the idea of the original word which is in the middle or reflexive voice). It is His sovereign choice to determine who will be the chosen ones. Romans 8: 29 states that whomever God calls, He justifies. In effect Paul says that God's calling of salvation to an individual will result in His justification to become a righteous person in Christ and in right standing with God. God will provide saving faith and redeeming grace to complete the transaction. That individual will repent, acknowledge his sin, and claim the blood of Christ for forgiveness to become a child of God. But notice that Paul does not refer to the individual in this verse. He uses the word "us." He has in mind a corporate body consisting of both Jews and Gentiles, which he enlarges on later in chapter two. Together these two races, and by implication all races of mankind, are joined together in the grand work of redemption. God has sovereignly molded together all those whom He has chosen to be one united body.

There is no indication in scripture that the choosing of a person for salvation by God is done apart from the will of the individual to accept and act upon that calling in His life. There is a heresy that says that a person is saved whether or not that person wants to be. He has no choice in the matter if he is predestined and elected before the foundation of the world. That is an extreme view of the doctrine of predestination and calling of God. We can consider the doctrine of irresistible grace in the believer's life, but at some point the individual must acknowledge his sin and the saving work of Christ to bring him into the family of God. Even though God may predestine and choose an individual, He will give the person a willingness to respond to God's gracious call upon his life. And why would that not be true? The offer of God is so great and magnanimous with generosity, that the individual cannot do anything less than accept that offer when God enlightens the eyes of his heart to understand this truth. To have God choose an individual, execute a plan to bring that choosing to fulfillment, and then offer that to the person would seem inconsistent for God not to put a hunger in the individual to refuse such an offer. This is the mystery of the relationship between God's sovereign plan for a life, and the individual's responsibility to conform to that plan.

Commentators make reference to the fact that God's choosing us is for a purpose known only to Him rather than choosing us in preference to rejecting others. When we think of choosing, we made reference above to the choosing of fruit, and our deciding on which fruit we choose, while leaving the rest for another to pick. God did no choose us in preference to another or above another since we are as sinful as any other person on earth. His choosing us is not a result of randomness, just as our birth and salvation are not some accident or quirk. The choosing is grounded in God's essential nature which is moral. It is certainly beyond our comprehension. We do not know why we are who we are, or why we are where we are. We can only acknowledge that God had something to do with that. He chose us for a divine and sovereign purpose. Kenneth Wuest suggests that God chose us, not as a choice in preference to not choosing another, but rather for the purpose of telling the Gospel that we discovered (or that was revealed sovereignly to us) to others so that they would not reject Christ. If this is true, then we see in God's election a foundational principle that is designed for outreach in content. We are saved to bring others to a knowledge of Christ so that God can draw that individual into saving faith and open his/her heart to want the Gospel of transformation to take place in that life. That is the heart of missions! We are born again to be soul winners, or at least witnesses whom God will use to proclaim the message of salvation to a lost world. We are called to be a blessing, even as Israel was called to be a blessing to the nations surrounding her (so Ps. 96:3, 10; 98:2).

In Ephesians 1:5, Paul says that we are predestined to adoption, and that it is according to the good pleasure of God's will. His will is in conformity with His predetermined or sovereign choices. The two are not separated. We see here a very beautiful characteristic of God in this verse. Our redemption is not something resulting from a God who has to reluctantly save people. He is glad to do it. It is from His good will. A holy God takes delight in pleasing to choose His sinful elect. How amazing! Some commentators even connect the last two words "in love" from verse four with the beginning of verse five, and so translate the passage "In love having predestined us." If that be true, we see even more God's willing design to save sinners as an act of love and not done reluctantly. Hendriksen calls it a "supreme delight" on God's part (Hendriksen 1967, 79).

In Ephesians 1:6-8, we see the grace of God bestowed sovereignly on His foreordained chosen ones. Our next section will deal with grace in more detail, but we want to reference that truth here briefly. All of God's plan of salvation in every aspect is His sovereign working. "His grace," "He made us accepted in the beloved," "In Him we have redemption," "Riches of His grace," "He made to abound." (underlines mine) This truth of the actions of God are carried on in the other verses as well. Just as Paul is repetitive in verse three using the word praise three times, so also is he repetitive here using the word grace twice. The translation is: "His grace, which He *graced upon* (italics mine) us accepted in the beloved." This emphasizes the unmerited favor of God to His chosen apart from outside influences. Paul once again shows the characteristic of God's love to His elect. The Lord delights to pour out favor on His favored ones.

In Ephesians 1:9-10, we see God's sovereignty in revealing the mystery of His working. Notice several things: His will devised the mystery. He laid out the plan for His own pleasure, and according to the timing that He thought best. He purposely orchestrated this mystery to work out a plan that he Himself thought best for mankind. The whole process is from God, and for God.

What is this mystery? Verse ten probably reveals the answer. But before we see that answer, we note that the mystery Paul refers to is not something unknowable, but something

"Undiscoverable through human insight or ingenuity and which God is now revealing through the Gospel or in Christ" (Longman and Garland 2006, 51). The mystery is the plan of God that He has for Christ to gather everything in the universe and transform it according to God's purposes so that Christ is all in all. The timing of this event is not chronological, or measured according to a calendar, but is a *kairos* moment, or a fixed time that God has determined in Himself to fulfill.

In Ephesians 1:11-12, we see another action begun with the phrase "in Him." This action is the obtaining of our inheritance as a body in Christ by God's predetermined plan. The verb Paul uses for obtained means to appoint or to be chosen by lot. In thinking of a lot, we usually associate that with throwing dice and whatever comes up is what we get. Not so with God. His lot choosing is far beyond our imagination. He did not choose us willy-nilly or with the throw of divine dice. According to His own just and integral determination He brought us into the family of God as His inheritance, consistent with His divine preordained plan for us as individuals and as part of the body of Christ. Notice that God willed it, and what He wills must come to pass. He willed it for His own glory. Combining the use of the word predestination in verse eleven with that of verse five, we see that God foreordained our adoption for His glory.

Before going on with some examples of the sovereignty of God, we need to point out a significant fact that is brought out in the Greek language from verses twelve and thirteen. In Ephesians 1:13, Paul makes the statement that: "having believed, you were sealed with the Holy Spirit of promise." Commentators make the observation that both of these words are in the aorist tense, and the passage could literally be translated, "having believed (participle) you were sealed *at the same time* (italics mine) with the Holy Spirit of promise." If we look at Ephesians 1:3-5, we can make a similar observation. In verse three, Paul says that God has blessed us. In verse four he says that God chose us. And in verse five he says that God predestined us. If we follow the same rules of grammar, we note that all three of these verbs are in the aorist tense. Taking those words together, and separating them from their adjoining phrases, we may translate these words as follows: God, having blessed us, chose us for Himself, having predestined us. We might even say that the blessings we have in the heavenlies in Christ are the fact of His choosing us for Himself and includes our predestination.

With God there is no time sequence. Everything to Him is in the "now." He is the eternally present One! Theologians attempt to place our salvation in some time sequence since we are time bound. We should not be concerned in which order God has chosen the believer, and where the terms foreknowledge, predestination, election, and calling all fit together with the salvation of an individual or of the Church. There are certain verses such as Romans 8:29,30 which may give us some indication of that. But do not get hung up on a theological conundrum that probably will not be solved, at least in this life. Just revel in what God has done in choosing us sovereignly from eternity to become a part of His family on no merits of our own, and with a purpose in mind that only He can define for us because He delights in us. It is all about God!

CHAPTER 3
EXAMPLES OF GOD'S
SOVEREIGNTY ON EARTH

It is obvious that giving examples of God's sovereignty over all things would lead us to an endless list of illustrations and a volume that is impossible to hold in our hands. We are dealing with Infinity, and infinity is boundless. Nevertheless, there are some things that we can state from Scripture that shows God's sovereignty.

1. CREATION

We read in Psalm 102:25 "Of old You laid the foundation of the earth, and the heavens are the work of Your hands." "Of old" refers to eternity, if we as humans can think of eternity and time in the same breath. God had always planned to create this world and the universe surrounding it. It was in His mind from eternity. In so designing this creation, God in His omnipotence, would have the say as to what was formed, how it was formed, and when it was formed. We do not have to get into the discussion as to the timing when it was formed. Depending on whether you are an old earth or young earth believer, an evolutionist, theological deist, or creationist, the range of time since creation began is from six to ten thousand years and up to fifteen billion years. For our purposes, the time factor is inconsequential. We are dealing with the fact that God is the Creator, based on Scripture.

The creation of God implies that everything has its origin in God which includes the inanimate (stars, constellations, and all that is associated with astronomy), heavenly creatures (angels, seraphim, cherubim, etc.), all animal and insect kingdoms on earth, microbes, as well as mankind. All that exists has been made by God or ordained through the laws of nature, which actually are the laws of God. The Scripture teaches that the world was made by God from nothing. We will look at this in more detail below. In fact God spoke, and the worlds came into being. "By the word of the Lord, the heavens were made, and all the host of them by the breath of His mouth" (Psalm 33:6). From these two concepts, we see that God chose to create whatever He wanted, and in the way he wanted them formed. This coincides with Psalm 33:9 which states, "For he spoke, and it was done; He commanded and it stood fast."

One of the clearest passages of the sovereignty of God in creation is found in the extended discourse between Job and God in Job chapters 38-41. Job is wrestling with God about the trials of life, and the reason why God has not revealed the answer for Job's heartaches. His friends do not have an answer for his questions. They only accuse him of sinning and incurring God's wrath. Finally God reveals Himself with a series of arguments that silences Job's queries. The following are brief portions of Job 38:4-7, 12, 31, 33, *Where were you when I laid the foundations of the earth? Tell me if you have understanding. Who determined its measurements?... To what were its foundations fastened? Or who laid its cornerstone, when the morning stars sang together, and all the sons of God shouted for joy?... Can you bind the cluster of the Pleiades, or loose the belt of Orion?... Do you know the ordinances of the heavens? Can you set their dominion over the earth?... Have you commanded the morning since your days begun, and caused the dawn to know its place?*

These are only a few thoughts that God displays to show His sovereignty in creation. The Word of God is filled with other passages that testify to the same truth. Job does not have an answer for life's trials, but he questions God's way of doing things. Is this not typical? When we do not know what is going on in our lives, we question the providence and sovereignty of God, thinking that if we can comprehend that, the trial will be eased. But would it? Take for example the fact that a person may know that he/she has cancer. That does not ease the pain and uncertainty of the person's future life. We can surmise what treatments may be necessary, and what the prognosis may be, either good or bad. But it does not answer the question "why do I have cancer?" or more pointedly "why did God allow me to get this disease?" We will never be able to answer that question any more than Job could understand the reason for his suffering. He believed himself to be innocent and should not have to suffer. God also affirms Job's innocence in Job 1:8.

God begins His discourse with Job showing His might and sovereignty in doing what he pleases, which no man can alter. In the remaining chapters and verses of Job, He also shows His hand of power in nature, and the creation and the manner in which animals conduct themselves in this world, all of which are under His sovereign control. God tells Job that He has created the earth, the seas, the sun (Job 38:4,8,12). But the Lord never does give Job an explanation for his suffering, and in the end, Job is content with that. He acknowledges the greatness of God and humbles himself before his Creator. We must conclude from this story that God can do anything that He pleases, and no one can stop Him. The psalmist reiterates this same truth "Our God is in heaven; He does whatever He pleases." (Ps.115:3) To deny this is to deny His absolute sovereignty in this world. Furthermore, we attest the truth that Jesus expressed in the Lord's prayer; "your will be done on earth as it is in heaven" (Matt. 6:10).

From a mission viewpoint, the majesty and sovereignty of God with respect to creation leads us to ask the question as to the purpose of God's work. The ultimate answer is that everything was created for God's glory. We will deal with that later. But the answer can also be tackled from another viewpoint which has an evident answer found in Romans chapter 1. Since God is the Creator of man, He desires to reveal Himself in such a way that man will respond to His acts. Romans 1:20 states, "Since the creation of the world, His invisible attributes are clearly seen, being understood by the things that are made, even His eternal power and Godhead (or divinity), so that they are without excuse." The concept of the word "Godhead" in this verse does not refer to the Trinity of Father, Son, and Holy Spirit. Commentators will acknowledge that it refers to a Being with divine attributes. Among these attributes is His omnipotence to create. God desperately desires that every person come to know and respond to Him in love and obedience. One of the most powerful ways to do this is to see Him in creation. Whereas there are many in this world with no knowledge of the Bible or of a personal knowledge of Christ, God has placed His creation as a starting point, so to speak, for all humankind to know who He is. This was evident before the Bible was written. The Bible tells us that people are without excuse. At judgment day they cannot stand before God and say that they did not know about Him. His sovereignty in creation includes a method whereby they can discover God, which can lead to a further revelation of God to the individual or group of people seeking Him.

In closing this thought of creation and the sovereignty of God, I am reminded of the song written by Mark Byrd and Steve Hindalong entitled *God of Wonders*, **Lord of all creation Of water, earth, and sky The heavens are Your tabernacle Glory to the Lord on High God of wonders, beyond our galaxy You are holy, holy The universe declares Your majesty You are holy, holy Lord of heaven and earth (2X) Hallelujah to the Lord of heaven and earth (3X) (New Spring Pub. Copyright 2000)**

2. MAN

In regard to God's sovereign creation of man, Psalm 139:13, 16 says, "For you formed my inward parts: You covered me in my mother's womb...Your eyes saw my substance, being yet unformed. And in Your book they were all written, the days fashioned for me, when as yet there were none of them." We often quote these verses in conjunction with the miracle of birth. But note that verse 16 states that God saw us before the mother ever became pregnant. He saw us as an unformed being! He could envision that someday we would be born in the circumstances that we are as male or female, with the parents that we have, with the talents and gifts that we are blessed with, in the social context of our upbringing and the destiny of our lives. In saying that, we have yet to come to the fact of sin marring His perfect creation, and the beauty He designed for this earth, and for us to enjoy that beauty before the fall. We will never fathom the greatness of God's sovereignty in creating man. The stars have untold numbers, the angelic world has untold millions, and every person who was born, has been aborted, or is now living, is known to God.

We will go into this more deeply when we deal with God's choosing us by grace for salvation. But Ephesians 1:4 reminds us that we were in the heart of God before the foundation of the world. Not only that, God has designed a plan for the people He has created. To illustrate this point, in speaking of Israel, God uses the three Hebrew words for creation in Isaiah 43:1, 7, "But now, thus says the Lord who created you, Jacob, and He who formed you, O Israel... Everyone who is called by My name, whom I have created for My glory; I have formed him, yes, I have made him."

The word for "create" (*bara*) in these verses means to create from nothing. The meaning of the word for "formed" (*yatsar*) is to fashion something from created materials. It is the external material. The word for "made" (*atsar*) in verse seven is to shape something. As an illustration, God makes a tree, and someone cuts the tree down to use a piece of wood. From that wood he fashions a table, chair, or whatever he chooses. In creating man, God has made him from nothing at the sound of His voice. In Genesis 1:1, we read "In the beginning God created (*bara*) the heavens and the earth." In verse 21, the Bible says God created (*bara*) great sea creatures. In verse 27, we read "so God created (*bara*) man in His own image: in the image of God He created (*bara*) him; male and female He created (*bara*) them." If God uses that word in these three verses, He is trying to make a point. Man is not the product of evolution, but of a direct act by God. We should note that these are the only three creations God made (*bara*) from nothing; the heavens and earth, creatures, and man. The scriptures do not record anything else being made from nothing. He then makes man and fashions him as He pleases from the dust of the earth. He breathes the breathe of life into man, and man becomes a living being, with a destiny, such as Israel had according to Isaiah, and such as every person on earth has. In all phases of his creation, man is under the direct control of God's sovereign guidance. In the Isaiah passage, God is not arguing against the natural means of procreation by a man and woman. He is attesting to the fact that He is sovereign in overseeing the creation of all humankind, and uses Israel as His divine illustration.

Not only has God created man sovereignly, but in His eternal plan He has created man in His own image. This is an amazing thought. We believe that God is self-sufficient, not needing anything or anyone. That includes companionship and fellowship. The Father, Son, and Holy Spirit were in perfect harmony and beauty enjoying their eternal relationship before the world was brought into being. They were self- sufficient and self-sustaining. But God determined that He wanted a creation whom He could communicate with and enjoy for His pleasure, someone who would acknowledge His status as sovereign, and who would love and obey Him. So He created Adam in His image; that is, with intellect, emotions, and will, and gave him a body, soul, and spirit. We will not discuss the arguments for dichotomy (man as a two part being of body and soul), or trichotomy (man as a three part being of body, soul, and spirit). There are solid theological arguments for either view. We only discuss the fact that God created man. H. Wayne House views the creation of man made in the *Imago Dei* (image of God) from four perspectives: the rational, spiritual, moral, and social dimensions (House 1991, 83).

In each of these dimensions in His creation, God had a sovereign purpose. Adam, the first created being, had a mind to make decisions. God told him to rule over the earth and have dominion over His creation (Gen. 1:26-28), and He allowed him to decide in which manner that command would be carried out. He also wanted Adam to have a spiritual relationship with Himself. God would teach him about Himself and the way in which he could increasingly become even more deeply in love with God. We might observe that this would have been God's highest purpose in His sovereignty for Adam and eventually all humankind to fulfill. What greater joy could God have than to see His creation hunger after Him and His character. God also made him morally responsible in obeying His command not to eat of the tree of the knowledge of good and evil. Adam's social relationship with God is seen in that God walked with him in the cool of the day in the Garden of Eden (Gen. 3:8). In creating Eve from Adam's rib, God also designed a social relationship between man and woman. We can imagination God asking Adam "well, how did it go today as you worked together in the garden with your wife, enjoying her company?" With this in mind, we also conclude that not only did God create man for His pleasure, but He created man to also enjoy the pleasures of God. One of those pleasures was a helper and wife. Viewed as a whole, we can affirm that God has created man in His sovereignty and for His own pleasure. But because of sin's effects on mankind, and because of the holiness of God, there is now a wall of separation that exists between God and man. God's pleasure for man has been thwarted by rebellion against God.

The challenge for believers is for those who have been called and redeemed by God to look on a world through God's eyes. What does He say about our situation? Second

Peter 3:9 states that the Lord is "longsuffering toward us, not willing that any should perish but that all should come to repentance." God created man for His pleasure, but that pleasure has been interrupted by sin. In order for a believer(s) or a believing church to be in harmony with God's sovereign purposes for humankind, they must look on the world in the same way that God does; that is, with a longing for humanity to be reconciled to God and to be restored to the pleasure of God by bringing lost humanity back into harmony with God's original purposes through the presentation of the Gospel.

3. SIN

Probably and arguably the most controversial aspect of God's sovereignty deals with the matter of sin and its entrance into the world. The cry of humanity is "why has God allowed this or that evil to happen?" There are horrendous acts of wicked men that seemingly go unpunished in the world. Tragedies occur for which we grieve and have no answer, except in many cases to blame God for allowing the tragedy to happen. We must answer the questions: Where did sin originate? Why did or does God allow sin to permeate the world? Is God guilty of wrong doing in mismanaging the world? What kind of sovereign God do we serve?

Although we turn to Scripture for answers, we do not have the whole picture because we do not have a complete account of what happened before and after the creation of the world. We do know that angels were created before the world came into existence. We know that God created the angels and all other heavenly beings perfectly. Ezekiel 28:11,16 says of a creature whom most biblical scholars believe is a picture of Lucifer, "You were the seal of perfection, full of wisdom and perfect in beauty...you were perfect in your ways from the day you were created." Apparently God had a special place of honor for Lucifer as "The anointed cherub that covers." What does that mean? The Old Testament describes the method by which sinful man was to approach God for forgiveness of sin. God commanded that a tabernacle be set up with varying sections and pieces of furniture. One of those sections was the holy of holies. In this place there were two cherubim made of gold who covered the mercy seat where the blood of atonement was sprinkled by the high priest once a year for the forgiveness of Israel's sin. The high priest would view these cherubim as he offered the sacrifice. Before Adam sinned, cherubim guarded the holiness of God's throne in heaven...Lucifer was probably the main angel who guarded the holiness of God and may have been the closest creature to Him in His creation, and possibly the most beautiful of God's created beings.

In Job 38:7; God Himself asks Job a question regarding His perfect creation. Job is puzzled about God's dealings with him over the events in his life. He asks where Job was when the "Morning stars (angelic hosts of heaven) sang together, and all the sons of God shouted for joy." This is a beautiful picture of what took place in heaven before God created the world and humankind. It was a perfect heaven.

In His sovereignty, God allowed the angels to have a free will, to make choices that would please Him and bring glory to Him. It is more glorious for God to give His creation the privilege of choosing Him rather than being created with no will of their own to choose Him over other things. So it was with Lucifer who chose to lust after God's position of authority, and in pride rebelled against him. In Ezekiel 28: 17, we read of Lucifer, "Your heart was lifted up because of your beauty; you corrupted your wisdom for the sake of your splendor." In Isaiah 14, we have a parallel passage to the Ezekiel 28 story. Isaiah writes in Is. 14: 12-14, *How you are fallen from heaven, O Lucifer, son of the morning! How you are cut down to the ground, you who weakened the nations! For you have said in your heart: I will ascend into heaven. I will exalt my throne above the stars (fellow creatures) of God; I will also sit on the mount of the congregation on the farthest sides of the north; I will ascend above the heights of the clouds, I will be like the Most High.*

From other passages, it appears that not only did Lucifer rebel, but a host of other heavenly creatures rebelled with him. The sin of pride to be like God in majesty and power got the best of Lucifer and he revolted. Revelation 12:7 states that the dragon and his angels fought against Michael and his angels. This passage probably refers to the end times when unseen warfare between heavenly hosts will occur before the Lord returns. But we note that there are a multitude of heavenly beings in opposition to God who war against Michael and his angelic force. Those were the angels who originally accompanied Lucifer in his plans to usurp God's sovereign authority. They would be the demons that are on earth today. Just as 1 Chronicles 29:11-12 displays one the most beautiful passages of the majesty and glory of God, so also the Isaiah and Ezekiel passages display the most horrendous insult to that Majesty. God gave Lucifer, now known as Satan, the privilege of exalting God, and he violated that privilege to insult God and defile His glory along with a host of other angelic beings. Any creature who does this is under the condemnation of God, and this indeed will be the final fate of Lucifer and his cohorts.

Did God know that Lucifer would act in rebellion? Undoubtedly He did since He is omniscient in His sovereignty.

Why did He not stop such an act of sin? Because God delights in willing obedience, not forced submission or robotic compliance, whether from heavenly or earthly creatures. In this regard we can say that God limited His authority and power to demand that Lucifer obey Him willingly. This is His choice to do since He is indeed sovereign and can demand anything He wills as good. It appears that in His mind, free choice to obey was better than the demand of obedience from Lucifer. The same situation can be said for Adam and Eve in the Garden of Eden. Did God know that they would sin in eating the forbidden fruit? The answer again is yes because God is omniscient. He wanted Adam and Eve to voluntarily obey His command not to eat of the fruit, more than He wanted them to be forced into submission and not eat. Thus sin entered the world through Satan's rebellion and Eve's disobedience which marred the beautiful plan of God to have a perfect creation.

Before we move on to another topic associated with the sovereignty of God, we should mention the decrees of God in conjunction with Lucifer's rebellion. The Westminster Shorter Catechism says, "The decrees of God are His eternal purpose, according to the counsel of His will, whereby for His own glory He hath foreordained whatsoever comes to pass." Notice that anything He decrees is for His own glory. We will deal with this in the third section. But there is a relationship between God's sovereignty and His glory. The two cannot be separated. Not only does God delight in willing obedience from His creation, but He delights in doing things for His own glory. If this be true, then somehow in His mind (and probably foreign to our minds), He believed that the decree to allow sin would bring greater glory to Himself than if He demanded forced obedience to His will. We certainly see the results of God's action in the work of Christ for our salvation. Did He allow sin as part of His sovereign decree in order to raise His Son to greater glory through His work on the cross and in the resurrection? We know that from Philippians 2:10 "That at the name of Jesus every knee should bow, of those in heaven and of those on earth, and of those under the earth, and that every tongue should confess that Jesus Christ is Lord to the glory of God the Father." In 1 Corinthians 15: 23, we read that Christ is the first fruits of the resurrection. Note the following verses that bring exaltation to God and the Son,

Then comes the end when He delivers the kingdom to God the Father, when He puts an end to all rule and all authority and power. For He must reign till He has put all enemies under His feet. The last enemy that will be destroyed is death. For "He has put all things under His feet." But when He says "all things are put under Him," it is evident that He who put all things under Him is excepted. Now when all things are made subject to Him, then the Son Himself will also be subject to Him who put all things under Him, that God may be all in all. (1 Corinthians 15:24-28)

It appears that the work of Christ will enhance God's sovereignty to allow sin to enter the world because it will bring the greater glory both to the Son and to the Father.

4. MAN'S CONDITION

As we have dealt with the fall of Lucifer and the resultant cause of sin in the world, now we want to hone in on man's condition, and his involvement in causing sin to occur in mankind. Just as God gave the original angels the permission to choose, so also He created man with the same DNA to oppose God's commands if he should choose to do so. The reason is the same as that displayed in the freedom of the angels: that is, God delights in willful obedience from His creation. In one of his sermons, John McArthur states that God does not cause man to sin under divine compulsion. Briefly stated, God is not the cause of sin, man is. He has complete freedom under the sovereignty of God to choose to act in the way he pleases. But if God is sovereign, does He not ultimately control man's actions? Yes! Did He not know that man would choose to sin? Yes! Did He not want to intervene so that the world would continue to be in perfect harmony with His plan? No, He did not want to intervene, or we might say, He willed not to intervene! We must also look at the act of man's free choice to rebel as controlled by God. And if God in His sovereignty allows man to have a free choice, there is no inconsistency to say that man, not God, has caused sin to enter the world. This is very hard for us to understand, but that is because we do not have the mind of God in His purposes, nor can we fully comprehend His sovereign will. We only see the result of His purposes.

Just as we cannot fully comprehend the will and purposes of God in creating man before his fall, so we cannot fully comprehend the condition of Adam and Eve before the fall from our sinful perspective. Various theologians will say that Adam and Eve were created innocent, holy, and righteous. Thomas Aquinas believed that righteousness was added after the creation (House: 1992, 85). Augustine believed that righteousness was part of the intrinsic original nature of man (ibid. 1992, 65). We do not know what it means to be innocent in the sense that Adam and Eve were. And we never will know that virtue (cf. Ps. 51:5). We can only understand the virtues of righteousness and holiness from the standpoint of being redeemed, and have God declare us righteous and holy (Rom. 5:19; 1 Pet. 2:9 et al). Whatever the virtues were before the fall, Adam and Eve lost them. The effects of their transgression have been passed down to us. And so we, like they now must travel the same route of having God forgive us and having Him sovereignly declare us righteous and holy.

In the fall of man, God viewed sin so heinous, that He would receive great glory in His sovereignty to rescue man from his condition. Adam was the Federal Head of all mankind. By that we mean that the entire human race was affected and infected by his sin (Rom. 3:23). His sinful DNA, so to speak, was passed down from generation to generation. Calvin views the fall from the aspect that each individual shares or has part in the sin of Adam, and thus individually inherits that sin nature (House: 1992:86). Adam and all mankind are now declared unrighteous and separated from God, both in fellowship and from Him eternally, and are dead in sin. Humankind does not have spiritual life residing in him (Rom. 3:10; Is. 59:2; Eph. 2:1). In Romans 5:12-21, Paul gives an extended discourse of man's sinfulness, with the inclusion of God's sovereign acts to redeem man. Paul states in Romans 5:12 that, "Through one man sin entered the world, and death through sin, and thus *sin spread to all men* (italics mine), because all sinned." This pictures man as a co-sinner with Adam originally. The verb for *sinned* is in the aorist tense in the original language. Some scholars conclude that the implication of this verse is that all mankind sinned with Adam, and not subsequent to him. Therefore sin is imputed to all of humankind since Adam is the Federal Head of the human race.

God hated sin so much that He moved in a such a way as to prevent man from bringing himself back into fellowship with God through his own efforts. As Adam and

Eve attempted to appear before God by their own standard or effort (fig leaves) to be in fellowship with Him, so it is today, and has always been. But God despises that. His highest creation is in utter ruin and chaos, and this is so horrendous in God's sight, He ordains to act in restoring His creation. This is utterly amazing! In His sovereignty, He allows man to choose his fate. Then He acts in the highest nobility to give man another chance to enjoy Himself on HIS terms, after Adam and Eve created such a mess. This noble act can only originate with God. Who only, but God, would sovereignly move to bring man back to Himself after the way man so disgracefully treated His Maker? It is a pure sovereign choice on God's part to intervene this way. The method He does this is discussed below under the topic of grace.

5. HUMAN AND BIBLICAL EVENTS

Along with creation and the origin and fall of the universe, we also can see God's sovereignty in the events of this life. There is nothing that occurs in this world that God does not know about, and in many cases even orchestrates its outcome. That is His prerogative. We must now deal with sin in this world in conjunction with the events that occur in life. We talked about God envisioning us as we will be on earth. Does He delight in seeing or allowing the tragedies that are in the world? Multiplied millions in the world are lame, blind, and crippled from birth. Multiplied millions are dealing with starvation, oppression, social injustice, sex slavery, and other ills of society. The inevitable question arises as to God's involvement in these situations. Did He create these monstrosities to occur? People ask these questions with the implication that God is either not loving enough to allow them to happen, or incapable of stopping them from occurring.

The answer is that sin has entered the world, and with it the corruption of God's perfect creation. We obviously cannot fully know the heart of God or His infinite feelings toward humankind. But we may imagine and fully believe that as God sees what He does in this world of heartaches and pains, many of which are not caused by man's violence, His heart must break on a daily basis. We would think that if anyone wanted to see the world come to an end and God's kingdom established, it would be God Himself. Add to that the events that are caused by people's sinful nature, the pain in God's heart must be compounded. Perhaps the only or main reason He acts in mercy toward His creatures, and does not hasten His own glory to appear and end the cycle of universal sin, is because He longs for man to repent, and gives him the opportunity to do so while He withholds final judgment on the sin cursed world (2 Pet. 3:9).

Moving from the general truth to specific illustrations, we see that God's sovereignty is involved in orchestrating events that occur in this world. There are many Biblical passages and stories that illustrate this truth. We can only choose a limited number. One of the most fascinating events under God's sovereign control is in relation to politics, and more specifically, the rulers of the world. Psalm 75:7 says, "God is the Judge, He puts down one, and exalts another." This refers to the rulers of earth. As you go through scripture, you see that God has sovereignly brought certain men into leadership for a distinct time and purpose to accomplish His will. For example, in Exodus 9:16, the Lord told Moses to say to Pharaoh, "Indeed for this purpose I have raised you up, that I may show My power in you, and that my name may be declared in all the earth." The word *purpose* is not in the original, but the verse infers that God brought Pharaoh to power at this time to reveal through him the entire series of events of the ten plagues that occurred by the hand of Moses and Aaron. He brings Pharaoh to power to show the futility of a human to thwart the plan of God, and humiliates Pharaoh and his army by drowning them in the Red Sea. The entire series of events are under the sovereign hand of God.

One of the most remarkable indications of God's sovereign hand in the events of kings is His relationship to Cyrus, king of Persia. We read these words in Isaiah 44:28, and the opening verse of 45:1, ***Who says of Cyrus, he is My shepherd, and he shall perform all My pleasure, saying to Jerusalem, "you shall be built," and to the temple "your foundation shall be laid." Thus says the Lord to His anointed, to Cyrus, whose right hand I have held to subdue nations before him .***

This prophesy in Isaiah was uttered in the seventh century B.C. The events of Cyrus' reign occurred during the days of the prophet Ezra in the sixth century B.C. Cyrus made a proclamation in 538 B.C. Ezra records these amazing words, "Thus says Cyrus king of Persia: all the kingdoms of the earth *the Lord God has given me* (italics mine), and He has commanded me to build Him a house at Jerusalem which is in Judah." Not only does God raise up Cyrus for His sovereign purpose, He gives the king the power to reign in Persia at this time, and the ability to do what God wants done in relation to Israel. He then communicates these exact wishes to the king. Through the king's decree to rebuild the temple of the Jews that the Babylonians destroyed, Cyrus carries out God's exact plan for Him.

Another illustration of God's sovereignty in Biblical events is the covenant that God promises to David. He gives the pronouncement that David will always have a king who will follow him on his throne. We read this in 2 Samuel 7:12-16, which is repeated again in 1 Chronicles 17:11-14, and reiterated by Paul in its fulfillment in Acts 13:23. God says to David, *When your days are fulfilled and you rest with your fathers, I will set up your seed after you, who will come from your body, and I will establish his kingdom. He shall build a house for My Name, and I will establish the throne of his kingdom. I will be his Father, and he shall be My son. If he commits iniquity, I will chasten him with the rod of men and with the blows of the sons of men. But My mercy shall not depart from him...And your house and your kingdom shall be established forever before you. Your throne shall be established forever. (2 Samuel 7:12-16)*

God is speaking of David's son, Solomon, who indeed did commit iniquity, as did his progenitors. But God said that David's throne would be established forever. He fulfilled this in the kingly line of the coming Savior, Jesus Christ. But Satan had other ideas about this promise. He attempted along the way to thwart this promise and destroy, or corrupt the godly line through his machinations.

The book of 2 Kings relates one of these devious ways in the story of wicked Queen Athaliah. The entire story is found in portions of 2 Kings chapters 9-11. Athaliah was the mother of King Ahaziah. She was the daughter of either wicked King Ahab of Israel, or of the wicked king Omri of Israel. There is uncertainty in the text on this point. In any case, there was a family tie between Ahaziah of the southern kingdom of Judah and King Joram of Israel Both went to battle together against Jehu who was commissioned by Elisha through the command of God to dispose of Joram and Ahaziah...Jehu carried out God's command. Athaliah now saw that her son was dead and proclaimed herself to be the queen of the southern kingdom of Judah. She now plots to kill all of the royal heirs of the southern kingdom, so that no one could claim the throne in place of Ahaziah (2 Kings. 11:1). In that way, she can take the throne of the southern kingdom as the queen of the nation. She believes she has killed them all, but did not know that there was one surviving heir to the throne. Providentially, Jehosheba, the sister of Ahaziah, and daughter of Joram, takes one of the royal heirs, Joash and hides him from Athaliah. He is secluded away in the house of the Lord, probably the last place that Athaliah would go, knowing her heathen beliefs. Joash is sovereignly cared for by Jehoiada, the priest, who arranges for Joash's inauguration when the boy is seven years old. Athaliah is slain by the soldiers loyal to Jehoiada and Joash. Jehoiada then mentors the future king until Joash becomes an adult and is able to rule on his own. As the only surviving heir to the line of David, God protects this little boy and preserves the godly line.

These three illustrations of God raising up leaders to fulfill His providential plan are just a few examples of His sovereignty in the political events recorded in scripture. Stories of this nature can be duplicated in non-Biblical events as well. Next, we will examine world events that have occurred which can only be attributed to the sovereignty or intervention of God.

CHAPTER 4
EXAMPLES OF GOD'S SOVEREIGNTY
IN WORLD EVENTS

A. THE AMERICAN REVOLUTION

There are many who believe that God's sovereign hand has been and still is upon the United States. From her beginning until this day, there have been accounts of "unusual" ways that God has intervened in America's affairs to save the nation from destruction. This book is not about America's history, but I use a couple of illustrations to show God's sovereign hand in the affairs of men. I am sure that authors of other countries, if their history would be viewed from a Christian viewpoint, could also testify to the unusual way that events unfolded in the affairs of their nations.

In his book *Seven Miracles That Saved America,* Chris and Ted Stewart relate the incident of George Washington's near tragedy in the battle of New York (Stewart 2009, 89-118). In reality, the battle of New York was the turning point of the American revolution. Washington was the commander of the rag-tag army of about 15,000 men with almost half not fit for battle due to sickness. Many of these men wanted to return to their farms to harvest crops. The British, on the other hand, were well trained and equipped for the battle. The Americans had no navy to defend the waterways of the

New York harbor. The British sent one of the largest naval expeditions in their history to insure the victory of New York. To add to General Washington's dismay, many of the people of New York were Loyalists to Great Britain. Two thirds of the property were in Loyalist hands. Added to the Americans' dilemma was the fact that the British fleet of some 400 ships and 32,000 men were well received by many of the New York Loyalists who greeted them joyfully. The situation seemed almost hopeless for Washington and his men. But God was to sovereignly intervene.

Washington sent General Charles Lee to set up a defense along the high bluffs of the entrance port to New York to defend the area against the British navy. A couple of British ships sailed up the Hudson River to position themselves against the Revolutionaries. The Americans opened fire, but their shells had no effect on the ships who continued their journey, anchoring where they could pick off enemy vessels that might want to re-supply the Americans with arms.

The date was August 21, 1776. A huge storm swept over the area with howling winds, lightening, and hail, causing houses to catch fire. Animals died who were out in the storm. Then the next day was clear, and 15,000 British troops came ashore. Five days later after planning their strategy, the British attacked the Americans frontally and from the flank. The Americans were overwhelmed by the British forces. This encounter ended in what could be termed a massacre. They soon realized that they had to retreat. The Army on Long Island had only one retreat route, and that was over the East River, where the British navy was sitting and waiting to catch the retreating army.

On August 28, the skies over the area grew dark, and rain began with temperatures dropping. A strong wind made it impossible for the British navy to move up the river to intercept the troops. Washington made the decision to move the troops across the east River that night no matter what the conditions of the weather, even though he thought it might be suicide to try the escape. In order to deceive the British, and because of the many Loyalists in the area, Washington planned a strategy telling his men that they were to attack. But in reality the Pennsylvania contingent who was with Washington was to maintain a rear guard while the others evacuated. The winds which were howling died down enabling the retreat to take place. The Americans silently moved equipment of canons and weapons, plus the men but did not move fast enough. The sun was about to rise, which would expose the whole ruse, and cause a massive slaughter of troops.

It was at this time that a dense fog settled over the Long Island side of the river making it impossible to see even at the nearest distance. As the soldiers escaped and crossed the river, they could see clear skies on the other side of the island, but the area where the troops were with-drawing was in complete fog. By mid-morning the evacuation was complete with Washington, and the last group rowing across the river. A short while later the British attacked the fort that the Americans had constructed, only to find no one there. The British were in shock as 9,000 Americans had safely fled the doomed area. George Washington's life was spared, along with his men, and the rest is history, with Washington leading the troops to victory and becoming the first president of the United States. Only the sovereign act of God could cause a fog to roll in at the right time and place rescuing Washington and his men from certain death.

B. WORLD WAR II - DUNKIRK

There were a number of strange and unexplainable events that occurred during the Second World War. William Breuer has recorded a number of these incidents in his very fascinating book entitled *Unexplained Mysteries of World War II.* The one I now refer to is perhaps common knowledge but extraordinarily intriguing. It is the amazing evacuation of Dunkirk during the period just before America entered World War II. In the battle of Dunkirk, thousands of British, French, Belgian and Canadian troops were cut off by the German army at the English Channel, and were destined for annihilation. Knowing their plight, an order was issued from Britain to gather as many small vessels as possible to bring the troops across the English Channel from Dunkirk back to England and rescue them from destruction. Every kind of boat imaginable was sent including fishing boats, yachts, ferries, and pleasure craft. Some 850 boats were assembled for this operation. Some vessels were brought from as far away as Ireland. May 26, 1940 was set as the day for "Operation Dynamo" the dynamo room of the British naval headquarters where the rescue plan was inaugurated. It is said that the Archbishop of Canterbury called for prayers throughout the synagogues and churches of England on May 26. Such was the urgency of the situation which called for national prayer. During the course of this rescue operation, two of the strangest events of the war occurred, allowing the "Miracle of Dunkirk" to happen; events that can only be attributed to the sovereignty of God in intervening on behalf of the allies.

The German panzers (tanks) were moving up from the south through France poised to destroy the allied forces. But they delayed their advance and did not move for four days. There were thousands of German troops also poised to attack the British from the north through Belgium. The British and French soldiers were completely surrounded and cut off from retreat. General Von Runstead, the commander of the German forces ordered that the ground operations of the panzers be halted, and Hitler agreed with the decision. Von Runstead's thinking was that the ground troops could defeat the British from the north. There was also an apparent miscommunication among the higher German powers that delayed their air strikes against the allies. It seems that Hermann Goring, the man in charge of the Luftwaffe air force, had assured Hitler that German planes could destroy the Dunkirk defenders and that ground troops wouldn't be needed. His thinking was that this approach could save many casualties for the Germans in a ground battle. This double delay gave the Allies time to organize an evacuation. Had the panzer units attacked, they probably would have virtually wiped out the entire army, since the German tanks had already reached the English Channel and were about 15 miles from Dunkirk. They only needed to close in on their enemies in a vice grip like operation. But it never happened.

The second "strange" event at Dunkirk was in relation to the planned evacuation itself and the weather conditions that "coincidently" occurred during the several days of the rescue. Herman Goering did not count on bad weather when he made his remarks to Hitler regarding the air assault. The weather conditions deteriorated, and the planes were never able to continue their assault on the allied positions. This gave the British military time to work their plan for rescue.

The operation to rescue the allied troops was planned for night. As the exercise began, a fog rolled in for several nights shielding the boats and troops from being seen in the process of evacuation. The small vessels which would be able to get close to shore, would move the troops out to the deeper waters where destroyers and larger ships were waiting to pick up the survivors and board them back to England. This evacuation ran from May 26 to June 4, 1940. Amazingly, over 198,000 British troops and almost 140,000 French troops in the nine day period of operation were rescued to live another day and fight to win the war. Many of these troops went back to Normandy in June of 1944.

Looking at it strictly from a human viewpoint, can anyone imagine not detecting more than 800 vessels in an ordinary rescue operation? Can you imagine soldiers waiting for hours in the waters of the Channel to get on board the rescue ships, and not have the enemy realize what was happening? Yes, there were casualties. Several allied navel boats were sunk, and those troops who were not rescued were captured by the Germans, (several thousand French troops) along with tanks and much heavy equipment which the allies had to leave behind in the rescue operation. Those troops who were not rescued surrendered on June 4. But in this amazing miracle, we see the hand of God, both in overriding human decisions, and controlling the course of nature to bring about His purposes in the war. But for His hand, this could never have happened. We must also believe that the prayers called for by the Archbishop of Canterbury played a role in this "miracle of Dunkirk." We can never separate man's responsibility from the sovereignty of God in either human or natural events.

C. WORLD WAR II - THE BATTLE OF MIDWAY

Just as God's sovereign hand of intervention was seen at Dunkirk, so also His intervention was evident when America became involved in the war in 1941. But we have to go back to Pearl Harbor to see the extent of His intervention before we can talk about Midway. Admiral Yamamoto, the chief military commander and planner of the attack on Pearl Harbor believed America to be a threat to her imperial accomplishments. He prepared a daring surprise attack on America's installations aiming to destroy the fleet at Pearl Harbor in Hawaii. If they could accomplish this, he thought that they would have about six months to conquer Southeast Asia before America would recover from this attack. The Americans were expecting the Japanese to attack the naval base in the Philippines, and never dreamed that the Japanese fleet would sail some 4000 miles across the Pacific and attack Pearl from the north. With their armada, one of the best in the world at that time, and in complete secrecy, on December 7, 1941 the Japanese sailed to within 220 miles of Pearl. Their planes took off from Japanese carriers to inflict horrendous devastation on the American base. Twenty four hundred soldiers were killed, 288 aircraft were destroyed or disabled, plus the various ships in the harbor including the USS Arizona. It was a complete surprise and a stunning victory for the Japanese. But they did not completely destroy the fleet as they had hoped to do. Three carriers and seven heavy cruisers "happened" to be at sea at the time of the attack. The fuel storage and maintenance stations on the mainland also were not destroyed by the Japanese bombs. Although they inflicted devastating casualties, they did not attain complete victory. When the Japanese air commander named Ginda assessed the situation, he urged Admiral Nagumo, who had led the attack, to launch a second attack immediately on the base to more completely destroy the military opposition. But Nagumo refused to do that. Instead he returned to the Japanese base because he did not want to endanger the Japanese fleet in the event of a counter attack. This hesitation on the part of Nagumo gave the US a second chance to prepare for further fighting and engage the Japanese navy at Midway. God had sovereignly prevented this second attack which would have devastated the remaining American fleet.

Fast forward to June, 1942. The battle of Midway became known as the "Miracle of Midway." Admiral Yamamoto believed that if the Japanese navy could have another confrontation with the Americans, they would cripple the allies and force America into a negotiation for surrender. His goal was to lure the American fleet into the Pacific and have the Japanese sub marines destroy them on the way to Midway and the Coral Sea. In preparing to leave, the Americans broke the Japanese code, and three American carriers with 180 planes were able to reach Midway unknown to the Japanese. On June 4, 1942 Japanese planes attacked Midway inflicting heavy damage. They returned to their carriers after a second successful bombing raid. Meanwhile, a squadron of American planes attacked the Japanese fleet and were shot out of the sky. But a group of American planes that had taken off from the U.S. carrier Enterprise somehow became lost in their attack on the Japanese ships. They were unable to locate the fleet and were lost in the clouds. At this time the Japanese planes were refueling on the carrier decks after their second raid, and the fuel tanks were scattered all over the decks of the ships as well. At that instant, the American planes broke through the clouds only to spot the Japanese craft in target range. Loaded with bombs, they attacked the ships and sent an inferno of flames into the air, destroying three of the four Japanese carriers and 253 planes along with their men. The Japanese were helpless to retaliate. In five minutes the war had changed, and the Japanese naval fleet would be rendered basically immobile. A "lost" group of planes in the clouds had sent a devastating blow and changed the face of the naval resistance.

The *Legal Dictionary* defines a miracle as "An event which is caused solely by the effect of nature or natural causes and without any interference by humans whatsoever." This certainly describes these war stories and other similar events in history. But we have to add another dimension. Who ultimately controls natural causes? God obviously does. We talk about nature as if it were a person. That is man's way to exclude a sovereign God from having control of this world's affairs including acts of nature. He is the One behind all events in the world. He is the one who sovereignly orchestrates the rise and fall of kings and empires.

D. PERSONAL EVENTS IN A LIFE

The sovereignty of God is not active only in the major affairs of a nation, as described above. As we think of God's activity in the daily life of an individual, we have to introduce the concept of providence which might also be considered as a synonym for sovereignty Providence is the attribute of God which describes His intervention in the affairs of mankind. Thus we can say that God's sovereignty and His providence both co-existed in the illustrations above. In the early years of our republic, many of the founding fathers were true believers in Christ. But there were also some who were Deists. That belief says that God started the world spinning and then took His hands off and removed Himself from the world. The end result is that man fends for himself in the affairs of life. He is free to do as he chooses, and to determine his own fate. Things just "happen." God does not intervene. As a result there is no such thing as miracles. There is no uniformity in the world. This philosophy or theology runs diametrically counter to Scripture in two major areas.

First of all, Colossians 1:16 tells us that the world is held under the control of the Son of God., Jesus Christ. Because God loved the world, He has a vested interest in His creation. He would never just start the world spinning, and then turn His back on that which He created. That would be just as ludicrous as if a mother birthed a child, and then, even though she loved that child, would abandon him/her in hope that the child would grow on his/her own. No, God desires to be vitally connected with His creation, and so will watch over the world according to His own character of infinite love and concern for it.

Secondly, there are a number of scriptures, especially in the book of Proverbs which tell us that although man does make decisions, God oversees the final outcome. Proverbs 21:1 says, "The king's heart is in the hands of the Lord. Like the rivers of water, He turns it wherever He wishes." Proverbs 16:9 says, "A man's heart plans his way, but the Lord directs His steps." God is not only concerned about His creation, He directly takes part in the affairs of the world. James Montgomery Boice has noted that God's providence is personal and moral and not abstract and immoral. With the foundation of providence in our thinking, we now examine the ways that He is sovereignly and directly involved with the affairs of people.

In the section below we will see how the grace of God plays a role in the events of our lives. But in studying the sovereignty of God, we also see how He either orchestrates or intervenes in the affairs of our lives. We are reminded from Galatians 4:4 that Jesus Christ was born just at the time that God wanted that event to happen. It was *His* perfect timing. We can say the same thing for the events of our lives. Not only are the details of our lives perfect in timing, but the manner in which these events play out is also under the Divine eye of God. But we should note that God may allow these events to work out in one of two ways.

He may directly intervene in a dramatic way, whether it be a healing of a disease, escape from an impending danger or death, or overrule in an event in which the outcome seemed to be different than what we would have expected. There are any number of illustrations we can give, and readers of this book can add their own stories of God's intervention in the circumstances of a life, whether their own or someone else's whom they know. But the bottom line is that God had a say in the outcome of that event. The great man of faith George Mueller of England operated an orphanage with a large number of children. Mueller's philosophy was never to tell anyone what his financial needs were to operate the orphanage but to tell God alone in prayer. He would be at the end of his resources when someone would leave a sum of money or food at his doorstep to provide for that day's needs. God in his providence laid it on the heart of some individual to be the channel of blessing to George Mueller.

But there is a second way that God's sovereignty is seen in life's occurrences. That is when He chooses for His own purposes not to intervene, but to allow the events of life run their course. He is as much in control in that situation as when He directly steps in to change the course of the event. That is because He is sovereign. Just as we cannot fathom the mystery of His choosing in salvation, neither can we understand the way He works in letting nature run its Course. For example, why does one person who has a fatal disease such as terminal cancer, be healed by God and have his life extended, while another person with the same disease dies? God sees fit to intervene in one situation, often with the aid of medical intervention, but does not intervene in another situation. Again, we have no answer except to trust a wise and loving God who "does all things well."

.

CHAPTER 5

PRAYER AND SOVEREIGNTY

One of the most practical matters that a believer faces is the issue of the sovereignty of God in relation to his prayer life. Why pray if God is sovereign and everything is already planned in this world, and in our lives from eternity? Can a person change the sovereign plan of God through his prayers? Maybe we should ask the question: "if prayer does indeed change things, do I want to change God's plan through my prayers, since He already knows what is best for my life and has a perfect plan for me, whereas I do not know the end from the beginning?" These are not just hypothetical questions. They are realities that many people struggle with in finding answers to this dilemma. Given all the events that may transpire over time, we could be praying for something that really is not desirable for us. If such is the case, will God overrule our incorrect praying to accomplish His perfect will for our lives?

The two illustrations above regarding George Washington and Dunkirk seem to show that prayer did change the events of this world. God honored the prayers of His people, and events turned out for their good. I am sure that many prayers of many people have resulted in God's blessing for them. But then, maybe God would have executed these plans whether or not they prayed. Truth to tell, we can only surmise the relationship between God's sovereign working in the world, and the role our prayers have in shaping the events of the world and our lives. But let's begin with a basic truth.

God has commanded us to pray. There are a multitude of verses that charge us to do that (1 Thess. 5:17; James 5:16, et al). Jesus uses the statement "when you pray" in the Gospels, especially in the Sermon on the Mount. He even gives us a model for prayer. With Him, it was not a question of whether or not to pray, but when we are to do it. It is a given that we will pray. Paul prays for others, and especially the churches to whom he writes (1 Cor. 1:4; Eph. 1:16; Phil. 13-4, and many other passages). He also asks that churches pray for him (1Thess. 5:25; 2 Thess. 3:1; Heb. 13:18, etc.).

The Old Testament gives illustrations that when men prayed, God answered their requests. One of the most obvious pleas for God's help was King Hezekiah, when the Assyrian army of 185,000 men were about to annihilate his country of Judah. The story is found in 2 Kings chapters 18-19. The king of Assyria's representative even boasted to the Jews that the God of Judah could not help them. Hezekiah in his helplessness calls on the prophet Isaiah to intercede to God on his behalf. The prophet reassures the king that all will be well, and that the Assyrians will be defeated. But Hezekiah also prays. Don't miss the plea that he makes which may be a hint in the relationship between prayer and sovereignty. At the end of his prayer in 2 Kings 19:19, Hezekiah says "Now therefore, O Lord our God I pray, save us from his hand, that all the kingdoms of the earth may know that *You are the Lord God, You alone* (italics mine)." God replies in 2 Kings 19:34, "I will defend this city, to save it for *My own sake and for My servant David's sake* (italics mine)" God desires that our prayers coordinate with His purposes, that people on earth may know that events could not happen apart from God's sovereign intervention. The result of this incident was that the angel of the Lord struck 185,000 Assyrians dead in one night. God did the work of defeating the enemies, but at least two men prayed for His help, and God coordinated these two events of prayer and deliverance.

The same principle of prayer and God's working occur when we sin. 1 John 1:9 is the classic New Testament passage that encourages believers to know that God restores our fellowship with Him through prayers of confession. But the story of David's adultery with Bathsheba and his confession stand out as one of the greatest examples of God's forgiveness as a result of a person's prayers. David went for a period of time carrying his guilt and putting on a front of innocence. The prophet Nathan confronts him with his sin in 2 Samuel chapter 12, and David acknowledges that sin. The two prayers of Psalm 32 and Psalm 51 show David's repentance and sorrow for sin. The shorter version of that is found in 2 Samuel 12:13, "David said to Nathan, "I have sinned against the Lord." And Nathan said to David, "The Lord also has put away your sin; you shall not die." David suffered the consequences of his adulterous affair, but was restored to fellowship with God as a result of his confession.

Perhaps we can summarize this relationship of prayer and God's working with the statement that God is the sovereign Ruler of the world. We have seen this from scripture. Therefore human prayer "seemingly" is not necessary to accomplish His purpose. But God has chosen man to participate with Him in doing His will by praying for the events that concern us. This is utterly amazing! He does not need us, but wants us to be part of His plan to carry out His decrees through prayer. We are instructed to prayer according to God's will, so that our participation with the Lord in prayer follows His purposes which He is destined to see fulfilled. This precludes that prayer is not answered and the destiny of an event fulfilled solely for man's purposes. A.W. Pink suggests that the expression "prayer changes things" should really be interpreted as saying that God changes things when people pray. We cannot persuade God to change His purposes. He is too wise to allow us to do that. His purposes are already mysteriously at work, but God wants us to join Him in carrying out that mystery.

We can be glad that God does not depend on us to carry out His purposes when we pray, apart from His sovereign plan. Just think of the mess we make if our prayers alone determined the events of the day or of our lives. How selfish we would be in wanting our way. How competitive we would be for our own glory as we expect God to work out our plan like some divine genie to please us. There is a distinction yet to be made between the believer and unbeliever regarding prayer. But even believers would fail in their desires to see a just world and a sovereign God move for His glory if our prayers moved the heart of God to act on our behalf apart from His sovereignty. We have reduced Him to a weak and whimsical god.

Therefore the first basic principle is that God has commanded us to pray, but it must be according to His will. Another basic principle is to distinguish between the prayers of a believer and a non-believer. If we are indeed to participate with God by prayer in carrying out His sovereign purposes, this pre-supposes that we are in fellowship with Him, or that we belong to Him as His saved children. It further pre-supposes that we have a desire to see God carry out His will and sovereign purposes for His glory in the world. The non-believer has no idea of what God's plan is for His life or for this world until he comes into saving faith with Christ. He wanders through life aimlessly, hoping that if he prays, God will hear Him. He has no assurance of this, since He does not know God personally. Does God have an obligation to hear and answer the prayers of a person who has no idea of why he is here on earth?

We can safely say that God does hear the one prayer of a sinner, which is to cry out for salvation. "Jesus, remember me when you come into your kingdom" (Luke 23:42) was immediately answered by the Lord, "Assuredly I say to you, today you will be with me in Paradise" (Luke 23:43). Every unbeliever who turns to Christ by faith for salvation will be heard. The prayer may not be complex or long, but it must be in faith and dependence upon the finished work of Christ. I submit that other than this type of prayer, God has no obligation to hear and answer the prayer of an unbeliever. If He so chooses, He may, and will do it for a higher purpose. The foxhole type prayer, "Lord if you get me out of this fix, I will do such and such" can be His means to awaken the unbeliever to faith in Christ, or at least to bring events into his life that may move Him closer to a decision. This reveals the mercy of God to an unbeliever.

The prayer life of the believer is entirely different. Jesus said, "If you abide in Me, and My words abide in you, you will ask what you desire, and it shall be done for you" (John 15:7). This and many other passages and promises are given to us to encourage us to pray with confidence, knowing that God will hear us. But taking our cue from above, the believer prays in harmony with God's will and desire that His glory be the preeminent purpose of his praying. This is implied by Jesus' words "if you abide in me." To abide in Christ is to seek His will for our lives and all that is connected with that will and purpose. Thus our praying is consistent with God's invitation to enter into prayer with Him to work out His plan for our lives.

The third principle, again implied from above, is that prayer is not intended to change the purposes of God. His purposes and our lives have been foreordained from eternity. Therefore our prayers are not to inform God of situations. He already knows about them. Matthew 6:8 states, "your Father knows the things you have need of before you ask Him." This is true in our lives, and in the world. But God does invite us to pray. It is pleasing to Him to have us ask Him about needs and situations. We make His heart glad when we seek Him. It is for His pleasure that we pray, because it shows that we depend on Him, and He loves that type of relationship. It takes the focus of prayer away from our needs, and focuses on His provisions. It magnifies His kindness!

What then is the relationship between prayer and the sovereign decrees of God? Arthur Pink suggests that prayers are part of the sovereign decree to work out His eternal purpose. When God calls or commands us to pray, in effect He is asking that we participate with Him in carrying out His plan for the ages, and particularly His plan for the individual life. The prayer of an individual does not alter the plan of God, but rather fulfills it. It is amazing to think that the prayer of a sinful (but redeemed) person can be part of the eternal plan of a holy God. And because God has laid out the plan for prayer, we can pray in full assurance of faith believing that our prayer will be answered.

This also turns the concept of prayer on its head with regard to our attitude in praying. God does not become a divine genie who answers requests and does our bidding. That type of prayer is saying, "my will be done." Rather we come to God with requests, leaving the choice with Him as to whether or not to fulfill that request. If we leave the prayer in God's hands, we have joy and assurance that all will be well. And this concept also changes the response to the following thought about unanswered prayer.

How often have you or I prayed for something and God did not grant it, even matters that we know God wants to see fulfilled, such as the salvation of a person, or the spread of the gospel in an unreached area. We know that God is not willing that any should be eternally lost. He has told us that in His Word. Yet unsaved are dying daily by the tens of thousands. How can we have peace, assurance, and gladness in prayer when we know that millions will spend their future in a Christless eternity? Why has our partnership with God in fulfilling His decrees through prayer not been realized? There is no clear answer to that question, other than to acknowledge that the responsibility to pray is consistent with God's purposes in this unfulfilled request.

If a person pleads with God for the salvation of a soul, the intercessor always has hope while that soul is alive, that God will answer that prayer within the bounds of His sovereign decree. But should that soul perish without the Lord, the believer must come back to the basic thought that God was delighted in the plea for the unbeliever's salvation, but to recognize that His decree is perfect. The Christian has fulfilled his responsibility to participate with God, but has allowed Him to be sovereign. We find a parallel thought in the book of Ezekiel 3:16-27. The watchman was to give a warning to save a wicked person. He was delivered from judgment if he warned the wicked person, and was accountable if he did not warn him. We should be burdened with the things that burdens God's heart, and in effect warn the person through prayer and witness if possible. The ultimate fate of the wicked is in the hands of a sovereign God. The ultimate human responsibility is in the hands of praying people. Together they make the purpose and value of prayer of utmost importance.

PART 2 - THE GRACE OF GOD

CHAPTER 6
GRACE - THE METHOD OF GOD
IN ALL THINGS

We have learned that the sovereignty of God is the overriding mystery and principle in the universe. God has the right as well as the privilege to orchestrate the events of mankind according to His purposes, and nothing or no one can hinder those purposes which He designed from eternity. Looking at it from purely a humanistic standpoint, that would make God an ogre to do anything He wants, and to use man as the puppet on strings to pull off anything He wants them to do. He has not consulted man or asked his opinion as to whether or not it is a good idea to do what God wants to do. That is the humanistic view that the unsaved world would tell you! But a closer examination of scripture tells a much different story. For the sovereign God of the universe is a God filled with love and grace, and in His kindness, He only has the best intentions for His creation. He acts toward His creation with the attitude of a heart filled with mercy, love, and kindness. This is His modus operandi. It is evident especially in those whom He has chosen for salvation. We are saved by grace, and we live by grace as believers in Christ. Just as

God proceeds within Himself to choose us for salvation apart from any merit of our own, so also He imparts grace entirely within His own choosing apart from any merit in the objects of those whom He graces. These are the two fundamental assertions to this section of our study.

1. DEFINITION OF GRACE

Let's begin with the definition of grace, and also see the ramifications in its broadest context. There are a multitude of definitions given by various theologians. The simplest and probably the most frequently used definition of grace is God's unmerited favor toward those who do not deserve it. But the usage of the Greek word for grace charis and its derivatives in literature outside of the Bible has a very wide meaning. It can mean a benevolently dispensed gift (Brown Vol. 2 1981, 115) to do something nice for someone else, to help someone weaker who is in need. In the apocryphal wisdom literature, grace is something that has been dispensed as a reward for good works. It is plain to see that all of these definitions fall far short of the biblical concept of grace. None of the above definitions outside of the Biblical meaning imply that the recipient of grace is unworthy to receive it.

The book of Ephesians uses the word grace 12 times. In his opening statement from Ephesians 1:3-14, Paul uses the word three times, once as a part of his greeting to the Ephesian Church. In the other two instances (verses 6,7) Paul uses the word as part of his glorious explanation of the work of God in salvation. But he also uses a derivative of the word *charis* in this section. In verse five, Paul tells us that God, "Having predestined us according to the good pleasure of His will" has done this "to the praise of the glory of His grace, by which he made us accepted in the beloved." (verse 6). The

Greek New Testament says that God did this "to the praise of the glory of His grace, by which He *graced us* (italics mine) in the beloved." Paul emphasizes the unmerited favor of God to His chosen ones. God gladly bestows His grace on His elect. Paul reminds us of the same truth in Romans 8:32, "He that spared not His own Son, but delivered Him up for us all, how shall He not also together with Him *graciously give us* (italics mine) all things?" The benefits of salvation are so over-whelming and stupendous, believers must extol God for His glorious grace. Grace is the foundation and fountain (so Hendriksen 1971, 71) from which all spiritual blessings flow. We do not know or understand why God graced us with this blessing. That was for Him to decide and is part of His sovereign planning. But we know that it is grace because it is a gift, and we cannot add anything to His gift. If we did, it would no longer be grace.

Paul goes on in Ephesians 1:7 to show that the forgiveness of sins is according to the riches of God's grace. Sinful man has been taken from the slave market of sin, bondage, and imprisonment (the concept of the word redemption), and brought to freedom in Christ. And how was this executed? A ransom was made through the blood of Christ, and in accordance with the riches of God's grace. If we summarize the thought, grace is God's modus operandi to bring about our relationship of salvation with Him. This is because Ephesians 1:8 declares that God made His grace to abound (the word means to exceed over and above) toward us. Hendriksen says, "The standard established by God's grace determines the measure of His forgiveness" (ibid., 83). Because God's grace is infinite, so also is His forgiveness.

With this explanation, we are now ready to give a more full definition of grace. I refer to Sovereign Grace Ministries for this definition, ***Grace is that unmerited favor of God whereby He in His own sovereign good pleasure, it pleases the Triune God to manifest His own glory by showing kindness and mercy to those whom, before the foundation of the world, God the Father chose or elected to save or redeem with absolutely no consideration or foresight of anything good in them.***

This definition sums up the magnificence of God's action toward men, and can only elicit from our feeble minds and tongues the praise and majesty that God deserves from us. The hymn writer of the song *Amazing Grace* says it all in the words, "When we've been there ten thousand years...we've no less days to sing God's praise than when we first begun." Indeed, when we have been there ten gazillion years, we will still sing of God's amazing grace!

2. GRACE IN THE OLD AND NEW TESTAMENTS

One of the sad misconceptions of Christianity by some people is that God dealt with people according to the law in the Old Testament, and by grace in the New Testament. Parallel to that is the concept that God is the harsh judge and ogre of the Old Testament, while Jesus is the gentle Savior and Deliverer of the New. First of all, in viewing the very nature of God, this concept is an impossibility. His character is consistently the same, which is holy, righteous, and pure. Malachi 3:6 says, "I am the Lord, I change not." The writer to the Hebrews tells us that, "Jesus Christ is the same yesterday, today, and forever" (Heb. 13:8).

God judges sin and righteousness in all ages in the same way. Since the Trinity consists of three separate but equal persons, the Father and Son, as well as the Spirit all act in the same way. Therefore to suggest that God is a Dr. Jekyll and Mr. Hyde is ludicrous. The God of the Old Testament is the God of the New, and He acts consistently with who He is. The character of God's attribute of grace in the Old Testament is seen by the various synonyms that are used in addition to the word *grace* itself. The Hebrew words are translated as loving kindness (Ps. 48:9), merciful (Deut. 4:31), goodness (Ps. 27:13), or slow to anger, such as was the situation with Jonah (Jon. 4:2). In all, these words are used as many as 80 times with many other phrases expressing the same concepts even though the exact Hebrew words for grace may not be used. With such lavish expressions of God's heart to a lost world, it is easy to see that the Old Testament is a book filled with grace, and that the concept of an angry, harsh God is unwarranted. Yes, He is angry at sin because of His holy nature. But He is also generous in grace because of His loving heart toward humankind.

To further clarify this with illustrations, we note that God is very gracious to His fallen creation in the Old Testament. From the beginning of human existence, God dealt graciously with Adam and Eve in the Garden of Eden. He gave them coats of animals to cover their nakedness, and promised Eve that a Son would be born from her seed that would save the world by crushing the serpent's head. Although the word grace is not used in that passage, it is evident that this is the modus operandi that God used to save the couple.

Before the Law was given, we see that God dealt graciously with Noah and His family. They found grace in the eyes of the Lord (Gen. 6:8) and God spared them from destruction when He sent the flood to destroy the world because of sin. After the flood, Noah makes a fool of himself by getting drunk and exposing himself to his sons. When he recovers his modesty, God blesses Him and Noah makes a prophesy of the promise of fruitfulness to his sons, who are actually the progenitors of the human race as we know it today.

In the days of Ezra after the Babylonian captivity, this priest of God leads the people and encourages them to return to the Lord and live righteously. They had fallen into idolatry causing God to punish them for this sin. Now they were intermarrying with pagans causing the godly lineage of the Hebrews to be defiled. Ezra turns to the Lord in prayer, and in chapter nine verse eight he says, *And now for a little while* *__grace__ (underline mine) has been shown from the Lord our* *God, to leave us a remnant to escape, and to give us a peg* *in His holy place, that our God many enlighten our eyes* *and give us a measure of revival in our bondage.* Despite the failure of the Hebrew people, God is still dealing with them in grace even though He must punish them for sin. Ezra looks to God to cause a revival among the people. At the end of the book, we read that the results of the revival were seen in the believing Jews separating themselves from their pagan wives.

One of the most precious promises in the Old Testament is found in Psalm 84:11, "For the Lord God is a Son and Shield; the Lord will give grace and glory; no good thing will He withhold from those who walk uprightly." (italics mine). This is a promise that any Old Testament saint could claim. The psalmist is referring mainly to the people of Israel, but his statement is broad enough to include all those who walk according to the ways of God.

One of the most beautiful expressions of God's grace is an expression which we use today in our church services. The so called "Aaronic Benediction" of Numbers 6:24-26 captures the notion that God is a God of grace in the Old Testament. Moses told Aaron to speak this blessing to the people, *The Lord bless you and keep you: The Lord make His face shine upon you and be gracious to you; The Lord life up His countenance upon you, and give you peace.* Matthew Henry observes that God offers His children His protection, pardon, and peace in this passage (Henry 1961, 148). Note what the Lord does for His people; blesses them, keeps them, shines upon them, is gracious to them, smiles on them with His countenance, and gives peace to them. God does this in light of the idolatry, grumbling, and discontentment that the Hebrews displayed in their wilderness journeys. What a display of grace in return for such actions! Some have made the observation that since the name of the Lord (Jehovah) is mentioned three times in the Aaronic blessing, this sentence structure may refer to the Trinity. How overwhelming and abundant God is in showering His favors upon His people in the Old Testament. The references cited above are only a sample of the acts of grace that God shows to His creation in the Old Testament. They prove that He is just as gracious here as He is revealed in the New Testament.

In the New Testament there are at least 41 verses that use the expression "grace of God" or "grace of the (our) Lord Jesus." A separate volume could be written on that phrase alone. The grace of God is more evident and dramatic in the New Testament than in the Old because of the work of redemption at the cross. The reason is that we do not see the full extent of God's grace manifested until we see it in Jesus Christ. For the same reason we do not see the full extent of God's plan to redeem the world until Christ comes on the scene. But nevertheless grace is at work in both eras, because the way to salvation is the same in both eras. In the Old Testament, a person comes to faith in God's promises, or to the extent that God reveals Himself and the person believes the statement or promise of God. When he does come to faith, God's grace is manifest in his life and that person is graciously received by God as His child. The terminology may be different, but the end result is the same in the Old Testament as a person placing his faith in the Lord Jesus Christ in New Testament phraseology.

3. HOLINESS, RIGHTEOUSNESS, AND GRACE

In order to tie together the topics of God's grace and His sovereignty, there is a consideration to observe before we can anchor these two characteristics together. We must deal with the aspect of God's holiness and righteousness in relation to our salvation and God's grace. Our thesis is that grace is God's modus operandi in dealing with humankind. But how do we deal with the truth that God is both holy and righteous, and we are both sinful and unrighteous? God's holiness can be defined briefly as His absolute moral purity and excellence. Because of our sinfulness, we are separated from God. He cannot have sin in His presence. We do not completely understand this when we realize that He is omnipresent, and therefore is present in the world of sin which surrounds Him. But there must be a barrier of holiness which in His transcendence ethically separates Him from His sinful creation. His holiness does not allow us to approach Him, and we have no merit of our own to close that gap which separates us from God. He demands: "Be holy, because I am holy." (Lev. 11:45; 1 Pet. 1:16). That is an impossibility, given the condition of mankind.

He is also absolute righteousness. His righteousness causes Him to deal with His creation in a just and holy manner. He has moral equity and does not show favoritism to His creation. He is the ultimate standard of right and wrong, and can never violate His code of moral justice. He has established this standard as His own code of righteousness, and His actions are consistent with that which He Himself has established (Ps. 11:7). True, because there is sin and injustice in the world , it appears at times that His righteousness and justice are not executed. But God is indeed working His plan which will ultimately reveal His complete righteousness.

His righteousness is seen particularly in His wrath toward sin and mankind. He condemns sin and judges the sinner. There is nothing we can do that can make us righteous enough to stand in His presence. We are not good enough to be in the presence of holiness, nor righteous enough to have a defense before that holiness. Any righteousness in ourselves is described by Jeremiah as filthy rags (Jer. 17:9). These two aspects of His character, righteousness and holiness, condemn us to eternal separation in hell. Unless God acts on our behalf we are doomed.

But praise God, in His unique way He bridges the gap between these two characteristics and our sinfulness, using two methods: the work of Christ at Calvary, and His infinite kindness to show grace to mankind. Jesus Christ, the spotless and sinless Son of God, takes on humankind's sinfulness, and in exchange gives believing people the opportunity to be seen as holy before God. Indeed, in becoming believers in Christ, we are now declared holy before God, because we obtain the holiness of Christ in our lives. I Corinthians 1:31 says: "But of Him are you in Christ Jesus, who became *for us* wisdom from God, and *righteousness* and *sanctification* and redemption" (italics mine). The word for sanctification is derived from the word holy or separate. When a person believes in Christ, he receives inherent holiness that places him in the same position as Christ Himself, which is holy before the Father. We do not have perfect or experiential holiness, because we still sin as believers who live in our sinful bodies. But in our standing before God, we are as holy as Jesus Christ in the Father's eyes . This occurs because God declares us holy, and can only do that by His grace apart from any action of our own.

There are a multitude of verses especially in the New Testament that testify to our holiness. We can't touch on them all, but in returning to the Ephesians 1:3-14 passage, we note in verse four that because of God's choosing us for salvation, we are holy. That is the only ground by which He can receive us into His presence. In Ephesians 2:21, Paul speaks of the entire body of Christ as being holy. In Hebrews 3:1, the writer of the epistle refers to the readers as "holy brethren." Surely, he is not referring to them as completely free from sin. The recipients of the letter to the Hebrews had problems wrestling with their desire to be identified as Christian believers when they wanted to return to the incomplete religion of Judaism and the Levitical system. They were waffling believers. But positionally they were holy in God's sight. We referred to Peter's exhortation above to be holy. In 1 Peter 2:5, the writer declares that believers are indeed holy. We are a holy priesthood, offering up to God sacrifices of praise. Our lives are considered by God as holy (see Rom. 12:1; Heb. 13:15). Note that all of these declarations of our holiness originate with or from the Father. The grace of God makes it possible for Him to recognize us as His holy people.

As we are declared holy, so also we are declared righteous. As holiness is inherent but not experientially complete, so also our righteousness is inherent but not experientially perfect. Our inherent righteousness is the righteousness of Christ imparted to us at salvation. Romans 3:10 reminds us that there are none righteous in this world. Romans 5:19 tells us that Christ's obedience to the Father and His dying on the cross was the means of our being made righteous. It was the righteous act of Christ to take the sin of the world, which only He could carry on Himself at the cross, that makes a sinful person to be declared righteous. Not only that, but Romans 3:25 states, "God set forth (Christ) as a propitiation by His blood through faith, to demonstrate His righteousness." The *Holman's Bible Dictionary* describes propitiation as the averting of God's wrath and justice (Holman 1991, 458). The Father determined that the death of Christ would divert God's judgment against us, and be the evidence that righteousness was made possible. on our behalf.

But it was more than just the cross that brought us into this righteous state. It was also the resurrection of Christ. "(Christ) Who was delivered up because of our offenses, and was raised because of our justification" (Rom. 4:25). God was pleased with the death of Christ, and so would declare anyone righteous who believes in that death and resurrection for his/her salvation. If Christ had not been raised up from the grave by the Father, that would have indicated that the Father was not pleased with Christ's sacrifice, and the process of the Savior's substitution for our sins in salvation would have been incomplete. But praise God, the Father was pleased with His Son's sacrifice, and so we have the gift of salvation, and all that is contained in His righteous act on the cross, and resurrection from the grave. Romans 3:24

uses the word "imputed." regarding our righteousness. We have nothing inherently good within us that pleases God. Unless God gives that gift of righteousness to us, we remain inherently sinful before Him. He does that by imputing or crediting His righteousness to our lives. Again, we see the grace of God at work in His kindness to give us this status positionally, and so enables us to stand before him, but only in the righteousness of Christ.

CHAPTER 7
EVIDENCES OF GRACE IN OUR
SPIRITUAL LIVES

We have seen that God is sovereign in the exercise and impartation of His grace to humankind. That is an axiom that cannot be denied from the Word of God. We have also seen how God administers grace in salvation. Now we want to examine the ways God displays His grace to the believer in daily living. Throughout Scripture, we see that we are bombarded with the evidences of His grace. Our first consideration is to learn that grace is the foundation of our growth in Christ.

1. GRACE AND SOVEREIGNTY

Having begun to detail the thoughts of God's grace as the method of His operation, we now ask the question: What is the relationship between the sovereignty of God, and the grace of God in salvation? We touched upon this briefly in the previous section. In one of his sermons Charles Haddon Spurgeon has written an excellent comparison of the relationship between grace and sovereignty. *First, then, DIVINE SOVEREIGNTY AS EXEMPLIFIED IN SALVATION. If any man be saved, he is saved by divine grace and by divine grace alone; the reason of his salvation is not to be found in him, but in God. We are not saved as the result of anything that we do or that we will, but we will and do as the result of God's good pleasure and the work of His grace in our hearts. No sinner can prevent God; that is, he cannot go before Him, cannot anticipate Him. God is always first in the matter of salvation. He is before our convictions, before our desires, before our fears, and before our hopes. All that is good or ever will be good in us is preceded by the grace of God and is the effect of a divine cause within.* (Charles Haddon Spurgeon, The New Park Street Pulpit, vol. 4. A message preached on August 1, 1858, at the Music Hall, Royal Surrey Gardens, cited by Warren Wiersbe, *Classic Sermons on the Sovereignty of God* Grand Rapids: Kregel Publications, 1994,114-115.)

This statement is consistent with our observations in part one in which God alone works His plan for each and every individual and for the Church of Jesus Christ. As J.I. Packer states so succinctly in his brief volume *Evangelism and the Sovereignty of God,* "Divine Sovereignty... embraces everything that comes into the biblical picture of God as Lord and King in His world, the One who "Worketh all things after the counsel of His will (Eph. 1:11), directing every process and ordering every event for the fulfilling of His own eternal plan" (Packer 1961, 9). How does He work? Here we can include the word grace as the modus operandi of that working out of His will. Just as God is sovereign in all of His dealings, so is He sovereign in His display of grace.

If we examine the marvelous verses of Romans 8:29-30, we come to a conclusion which at first is not evident, but is implied. Paul says, *For whom He did foreknow, He also predestined to be conformed to the image of His Son, that He might be the firstborn among many brethren. Moreover, whom He predestined, these He also called; whom He called, these He also justified; and whom He justified, these He also glorified.*

This is the sovereign plan of God for His elect. But in order for God to accomplish this goal, He would have to impart His grace, since He knew that the world He created would fall into sin, and He would have to overcome that sin. We saw above how He did this that through the work of Christ in His death and resurrection. Romans 8:29 says that God called us. How did he do that? We had to make a conscious decision to accept that call. But because of sin and deadness to God (Eph. 2:1), we are unable to answer that call in our own ability. Here God enables us to respond to that call by His grace making that call to us effective or possible. He awakens the heart of the unbeliever in a sovereign way to hear that call. This is the basis of Paul's thinking in Ephesians 2:8-9; saved by grace through faith, the working of God, and not of ourselves! The actions of God in Romans 8 are supplemented by the grace of God as seen in Ephesians 2. Grace and sovereignty go hand in hand; sovereignty the plan, grace the modus operandi. In fact, we might say, as John Murray does, "(Grace) is the link between the call and the response on the part of the person called" (Murray 1961, 64).

2. GRACE IN SANCTIFICATION

There are many Christians who will testify to the truth that we are saved by grace alone. But not having been taught the basic doctrine of the Gospel, they will go on believing that they must live, and yes struggle in the Christian life on their own. They may know that Christ is with them, and if they surrender their lives to the Lord, they will overcome sin and temptation. All that is true. But they are not cognizant of the fact that the Christian life is made possible by the grace of

God. They miss out on the joy of knowing that the Christian life is totally all about a life of grace. There is grace that saves, and grace that keeps! They are not aware that they can only live the Christian life by the grace that God gives them in order to fulfill His calling for their lives. Some also are unaware that they cannot earn grace. It is as though they think that good works result in the grace that God gives them for Christian living. Or to put it another way, they believe that they are saved by grace and sanctified by works. Not so!

Sanctification is the doctrine which says that the believer is set apart for God. This work is accomplished by the indwelling Holy Spirit Who sets us apart to God. Paul expresses this in Romans 6 as having died to sin or having been crucified with Christ in His death; (Rom. 6:6, 8). The believer has been given the new nature of God Himself (2 Cor. 5:17), and has been freed from the power of sin that expresses itself daily in the sinful body (Rom. 6:9). He is primarily desirous of becoming more like Christ as he grows in the Christian life. If that latter goal is not the heartbeat of a person, then he is not a true born again believer. This is not the venue to completely discuss that concept, but the apostle John states as much in his first epistle (1 John 2:15, et. al).

How does the above facts of the Christian life play out in daily living? The answer is grace! In our natural desires, we would tend to live a life that pleases ourselves. Not only that, we might tend to think that we can sanctify ourselves, or if you please, live the Christian life on our own so that we would be seen as the ones having the strength to overcome sin. That is nothing more than pride. And pride always opposes grace.

When the Holy Spirit enters the life, the basic viewpoint of our lives is changed. Whereas once we delighted to have sinful thoughts and actions, now we hate sin, and delight to do the things that please God (1 Cor. 2:14-16). This is impossible to happen unless the grace of God sends the Holy Spirit to change our values through the new life God has given us. One of the most important values the Spirit places within us is humility. Humility says "I can't but God can!" If the Spirit did not do this, we would be incapable in ourselves to overcome the stronger work of Satan, who wants us to fail in our Christian lives. Someone has suggested that that we inherit the power to be a child of God and are equipped to be holy through the grace of God . Paul sums up this transformation that takes place in our lives in 2 Cor. 3:18, "We...are being transformed into the same image from glory to glory, just as by the Spirit of the Lord."

One of the greatest areas of life which needs the grace of God for sanctification is in the mind. 2 Corinthians 10:5 says, "Casting down imaginations (NKJV arguments) and every high thing that exalts itself against the knowledge of God, bringing *every thought into captivity* (italics mine) to the obedience of Christ." If Satan wants to do any one thing in our lives, it is to rule the mind, because from the mind comes evil thoughts and sinful actions that cause our spiritual downfall (Cf. James 1:14-15). And since Satan is more powerful than we are, he will win every time, because the mind, like every other part of our body, is subject to the fall and its results. God must do His work in our minds. The wonderful news is that He wants to do just that. When we are born again, and the Holy Spirit comes to indwell us, there is a complete change of mind, purpose, intent and disposition of our being. Jeremiah 31:33 puts it this way: "I will put my laws in their minds, and write it on their hearts." Ezekiel says basically the same in Ez. 36:26,27, *I will give you a new*

heart and put a new spirit within you; I will take the heart of stone out of your flesh and give you a heart of flesh. I will put My Spirit within you and cause you to walk in My statues, and you will keep My judgments and do them. Both Jeremiah and Ezekiel are referring to the day when Israel will be completely changed from the rebellious people they are to become the obedient people of God. Although this refers to an Old Testament prophesy yet to be fulfilled, the principle of a complete change of heart and life is applicable for us today. God renews our hearts and minds to desire His will for us when He regenerates us.

It is that same work of God's grace that allows His power to flow through us. As believers in Christ, we do not need to despair or lose hope that our minds and thoughts will be dominated by sinful desires. That power of God graciously given to us is greater than Satan's power to dominate us. We claim that power to overcome by faith and the acknowledgement that God's Word is true: i.e. "Greater is He who is in you than he who is in the world." (1 John 4:4). John Murray makes a very cogent observation in his book R*edemption-Applied and Accomplished*, "It is one thing for sin to live in us: it is another for us to live in sin. It is one thing for the enemy to occupy the capital: it is another for his defeated hosts to harass the garrisons of the kingdom." (Murray 1961, 145). The sin that lives in us attempts to dominate our minds. Praise God His power enables us to live daily in the victory He supplies by His grace.

One of the joys a believer learns is that grace in sanctification takes the pressure from him to be holy, and places it squarely on God to transform him. Who is more capable than God to make that happen? The believer does not have to "fake it" in his Christian life. It is not his life, but

Christ living in and through him by His grace. Paul states that truth in Galatians 2:20, "It is no longer I who live, but Christ lives in me: and the life which I now live in the flesh, I live by faith in the Son of God." This truth also gives the believer the liberty to enjoy God to the extent that He wants him to enjoy the Lord. Therefore in enjoying Him, he brings praise to the Lord, as well as show a testimony of Christ's grace to the world around him.

3. GRACE, LAW, AND LEGALISM

Many authors have written volumes quite exhaustively on the topic of law and grace. There is no need to go into any great length or to repeat what very competent scholars have written. The purpose here is to briefly state that grace is God's modus operandi in dealing with humankind, and the law can be seen as a "seeming" deviation of grace which man uses to attain a right or better standing with God. There are also many aspects in discussing the Old Testament law, and its relationship with legalism. What is the place of the Ten Commandments in our lives today? Is there a place for a legalistic system of living that a believer in Christ may employ in his daily walk? Will this help him to find favor with God?

We should note that the Ten Commandments are still valid today, as they were when God gave them to Moses. All Ten Commandments are found in the New Testament, except the direct command to observe the Sabbath (Saturday). But there is a command to observe the Lord's day (1 Cor. 16:1-2). We conclude that the Ten Commandments are God's universal decree and apply also for this day and age, although they may not be expressed as the original Ten Commandments that God gave to Israel.

What is the believer's responsibility to these commands under grace? James tells us that in breaking one law, a person breaks them all (James 2:10). As an illustration, if a chain of several links is broken in one place, the chain is no longer useful even though the other links are still in tack. The New Testament believer cannot keep the Ten Commandments, or any of the other Old Testament laws, just as the Old Testament saints could not keep them. The good news is that Christ, being sinless, has kept every law and fulfilled every part of the Old Testament requirements which humankind could not fulfill. In doing this, Christ's righteousness has been credited to us (Rom. 3:22; :4) since He indwells believers. Therefore believers are free from the guilt and condemnation of the Law, including the Ten Commandments. Paul refers to the Law in Galatians telling us that it brings bondage. But he states in Galatians 3:6, "Because you are sons, God has sent forth the Spirit of His Son into your hearts, crying out "Abba, Father!" Therefore you are no longer a slave but a son, and if a son, then an heir of God through Christ."

Believers in Christ live by grace because of the indwelling Spirit. They are able by the Holy Spirit to obey these commands, albeit not perfectly because they still retain the sinful effects of the fall in their bodies. They are not condemned by the law and commandments as a person would be during the time of the Old Testament. Christ has fulfilled these commandments, and the ceremonial law, making it possible for them to be free from the law's condemnation, and at the same time living under the law of Christ (Rom. 10:4).

While briefly touching upon our discussion of the Old Testament Law, we turn next to the consideration of the believer's walk with Christ as it relates to legalism. This can be considered as an extension of the previous topic of grace and sanctification. I want to use a personal experience to bring this topic into relevance. When I was growing up in the 1940's and 50's, there was much talk in the Church about the so-called negative aspects of Christian living. Things like *The Seven Deadly Sins* was popular. I was saved at the age of twelve. We were not supposed to go to movies, dances, smoke cigarettes, play cards, gamble, bet on horse races, and a lot of other activities that would be considered improper or sinful. A person's spiritual standing was judged by what he did or did not do. I failed to live up to those standards as a young believer. I loved to go to movies as a kid and played both cards and dice for money! As I reflected back on those days, I think that my desire was to please God in what I thought was proper conduct for me, and I do not recall being particularly convicted about these actions. After I fully surrendered my life to Christ in my late teens, I avoided these activities, perhaps because I was more mature. I was considered to be a "spiritual kid" by my many unsaved friends because of my relationship to Christ which they observed in me, and not by what I did or did not do according to church standards. What mattered to me was whether or not I was pleasing God. My principle was (and still is!) not to see how close I could get to sinning or being worldly without crossing the line. It was to see how far away I could stay from sin and maintain my daily walk with God. I did not realize my immaturity at that time, but it was the grace of God that was working in my heart to desire this goal for my life. I was not trying to repay Him for what He had done in saving me, but simply to live the Christian life because I loved Him. I wanted to be conformed to the image of God's Son, and His grace was helping me to achieve that by putting His desires into my heart.

How does legalism and keeping the law, or any set of rules play into this scenario? Simply stated; we are saved by grace, and we live by grace! Any attempt for a believer to live otherwise is to insult the work of God in salvation. Furthermore, Scripture is clear that any law or set of regulations is completely impossible in the least to produce godliness in that person's life. John Reisinger, in his on line sermon entitled *Sanctification by Grace* has put it very succinctly, "If grace does not conquer sin, then I am not any better off than I was under the law." To attempt to keep a set of rules is in effect to pay back God for the debt we owe Him for our salvation. This has at least two fallacies; we can never repay Him for what He has done on our behalf, and even if we could, we would never know or be able to calculate how much repayment would be enough. If believers fall into the trap of living to repay their debt to God, they will always be wrestling with shortcomings and the thought that God is angry with them. They haven't done enough to please Him. They live in guilt, and may even wonder if they are saved. Until the believer realizes that he must come to the end of himself/herself and cry out to God in effect by saying "the Christian life for me to live is impossible, I need Your help," that person will struggle spiritually the entire life. But when the believer does come to that realization and confession of helplessness to live the Christian life, God will intervene by pouring our His grace on that life. Romans 4:5 sums it up nicely, "To him who does not work, but believes on Him who justifies the ungodly, his faith is counted for righteousness." This is not only true for coming to Christ in salvation, but living in Christ for victory.

It is easy for believers to think that they can win God's favor by the things they do. That becomes what is called "performance oriented" in the Christian life. We must be reminded that, according to Galatians 2:20, Christ lives in the believer. The believer is dead with Christ, therefore anything he does in the flesh cannot please God. But his pride allows him to think that he can do something to win God's favor. The Christian must be reminded from Scripture that God will not love him/her any more when that person attempts to win His favor by works, nor will He love him/her any less when the person fails in his/her Christian life. That is the beauty of God's grace. It is all about God, and not about us or our strivings. Pushing the point further, believers do not receive more of God's grace if they maintain a daily devotional life or attend church faithfully. They may grow in knowledge and understanding about God's grace with these exercises, but God does not reward them with "extra grace" because of performing these spiritual activities. That would amount to works sanctification, and that is impossible in God's economy.

But there is another aspect to this thought as well. Along with realizing that we can never do enough to please God, it is liberating to know that we do not have to do anything to please Him with our efforts, but only to live in the atmosphere of His unmerited grace. This gives joy in salvation, not fear of failing to attain to any standard that will result in God's favor. Going back to my childhood experiences, I had the concept of wanting to please God by avoiding sinful pleasures, and not count that as a burden. I did want to bring joy to the Father's heart and sense His pleasure. Had I unconsciously believed that I was gaining grace in my sanctification as I separated myself from worldly temptations (I may have done that and not been aware of it), how wrong I was! Christ's grace was always present in my life. He was not increasing or decreasing His grace in my life depending upon good or bad behavior.

John Piper has written a very insightful book entitled *Future Grace*. He deals with this topic from the perspective of gratitude. The word *gratis* is found in this word. The fact that God's grace is free should well up a spirit of gratitude in our hearts . We praise God for what He has done in the past, and this prompts us to trust Him by faith to pour out His continuous grace on the events of our lives in the future. We do not attempt to repay God, (or as Piper would say, have a "debtor's ethic") because that defeats the purpose of gratitude, and causes us to fall into the attitude of repaying a debt to Him, something which is heinous to God. Therefore we live and give gratitude to God as an evidence of faith that He will supply our needs by His grace for tomorrow. To quote Piper, *Faith in future grace is the secret that keeps impulses of gratitude from turning into the debtor's ethic. True gratitude exults in the riches of God's grace as it looks back on the benefits it has received. By cherishing past grace in this way, it inclines the heart to trust in future grace. We might say that gratitude has a strong appetite for the enjoyment of looking back on the outpourings of God's grace. (Piper 1995, 38).*

In his section on A Tribute to Gratitude, Piper emphasizes this thought as he states, There is a sense in which gratitude and faith are interwoven joys that strengthen each other. As gratitude joyfully revels in the benefits of past grace, so faith joyfully relies on the benefits of future grace. Therefore when gratitude for God's past grace is strong, the message is sent that God is supremely trustworthy in the future because of what He has done in the past. (ibid., 48).

In conclusion, keeping the Law, or any set of rules outside of the Bible to increase our standing before God is futile. God is not pleased, and we are frustrated in our Christian living, leading to a life of defeat and introspection. Only grace can help the believer to live the life that glorifies God.

4. GRACE AND SINNING

From the above discussion, it is quite plain that God owes us nothing. Anything that He does toward humankind is from His loving heart. We are saved by grace and we live as believers moment by moment by grace! One of the greatest evidences of God's grace is His forgiveness in the life of a believer. No matter how much we revel in, meditate on, and live by grace, we still live in fallen bodies and commit sin. 1 John 1:8, 10 clearly affirm this, "If we say that we have no sin, we deceive ourselves, and the truth is not in us....If we say that we have not sinned, we make Him a liar, and His Word is not in us."

We do not want to spend a lot of time on the topic of Romans chapter 6 and the question of deliberately sinning to allow grace to abound. Believers have answered that question in their hearts by saying that they will not intentionally live in sin. But there is a seminal truth which is expressed very succinctly by Bryan Chappell in his book *Holiness By Grace,* "Sin does not create our identity. Our lives are hid in Christ (Col. 3:3); we are characterized by righteousness (Phil. 3:9)" (Chapell 2001, 50). The believer's heart is riveted on the grace of God to enable him to live the way God transformed him to live, which is "To produce good works which God prepared beforehand that we should walk in them." (Eph. 2:10). This is at the core of his being. Grace is so at work that the believer has no delight to walk in darkness, but delights in the light (1 John 2:8). As we live in the light, God's grace is provided to help us to overcome the evil that surrounds us.

Nevertheless, we must make room for a brief discussion concerning the believer who does sin. In his book *The Cost of Discipleship* by Dietrich Bonhoffer, the author makes reference to what he calls "cheap grace." In essence he says that because Christ paid for our sins, all that we have in Christ can be had for nothing. Carrying that to its logical conclusion, a person can live in grace as freely as he/she chooses and count on Christ's work of grace to cover the sins. This concept diminishes the seriousness of sin, and makes the work of Christ look cheap. Paul does not explain it exactly in this way in Romans chapter six, but this is the heart of his cry; "Shall we continue in sin that grace may abound?" (Rom.6:1) His resounding answer is "Certainly not" (Rom.6:2), or as another translation says "let it not be!" God's character would never allow a person to believe that what God has so freely granted to him, i.e. salvation and grace, can be used to live a life that is absolutely contrary to His holy character. There is no room for deliberate, habitual sinning in the believer's life.

Having said that, the believer must still face his own humanness and deal with his failures. What is the answer to those failures? The same answer as before, grace! The only way to deal with sin in the life is to be truthful. God expects honesty with us. If we are willing to be honest, He is willing to be gracious and forgiving. That forgiveness is not based on what we can do except to acknowledge and confess that failure, and rely on the work that Christ has done in redeeming us. He has completely covered every sin that we have done, and every sin that we will do in the future, including present sin. This is the essence of 1 John 1:9. If we confess, or tell

God the truth about our sin (which He already knows, but wants us to acknowledge), He is prepared to forgive. There is no merit on our part or anything that we can do to earn that merit of forgiveness. It is solely of His grace to restore the fellowship that we have destroyed through sin. What is marvelously amazing is the wonder that God is willing to continuously forgive. He told Peter that when a person sins against us, we are to forgive him seventy seven times (or as some versions say seventy times seven) (Matt. 18:22). We are to forgive so often that we can't count or remember the times that we have forgiven a person. Thus it is with God. He has forgiven us multiple seventy times seven sins that we have committed against Him. In truth, He is more anxious to forgive and restore our relationship with Him than we are willing to come back to Him. How often does the believer continue in his sin, and rob God of the joy in bringing him back to close fellowship through confession and forgiveness. He is like the father of the Prodigal Son waiting for us to repent and confess that we have fallen short of His expectations for our lives. The truth to remember is that God never gives up on us. Sometimes believers give up on themselves because of their lack of overcoming sin in their lives. But God does not look at us in this way. He sees a child of God who belongs to Him, "accepted in the beloved" (Eph. 1:6), and one whom He will never stop loving.

1 John 1:9 says that God is faithful and just to forgive. We experience the heart of the Father. But we also say this reverently, and not being presumptuous; God's nature of justice and faithfulness requires Him to forgive based on confession of sin. He must be gracious to restore or He is not faithful to His Word, or just in acknowledging the death and resurrection of Christ for the sin of mankind which is

the basis for the forgiveness of sin. We might say that this is forgiveness from the Divine aspect. God set the parameters of forgiveness in eternity past in His sovereign planning of redemption. Now He must fulfill that plan by acting in accordance with what He planned. But as we learned above in the study of sovereignty, He does this because He is also gracious as well as faithful and just. He delights to forgive! He delights to restore. He delights to re-create! And mankind is the beneficiary of His graciousness.

CHAPTER 8
EVIDENCES OF GRACE
IN DAILY LIVING

1. GRACE AND DECISION MAKING

There are any number of examples or evidences that we can use to show the grace of God in our daily living. The ones chosen are only to illustrate the truth of God's grace, and by no means are they exhaustive (indeed, we cannot exhaust His grace!). But before we get into some practical examples, let's set forth an overall principle. The principle was first explained to this author in reading the two volumes of Hudson Taylor's life. The shorter version of his life is found in the book *Hudson Taylor's Spiritual Secret*. Actually, it is no secret but a biblical principle that every believer ought to embrace. Taylor called it the "exchanged life." When he was beginning to establish the China Inland Mission, he wrestled with the enormity of that task. He also wrestled with God about doing what he believed God wanted him to do, and his inadequacy in accomplishing God's will. One day he went to Brighton Beach in England and poured out His heart to God in prayer. The answer came back to him that it was God, not Taylor, who would establish the work. Taylor had to "let go and let God" as the expression says, and rest his soul in the hands of God. He did this, and the release from the burden of his task was immediate. Taylor realized that in surrendering to God, and allowing Christ to live out His life in Taylor, he was now going to enjoy the benefits that God by grace was about to pour out on his life. This is exactly what God wants to do in every believer every moment of every day. Although this truth was stated above, we come back to it again. It is the principle found in Galatians 2:20, "I am crucified with Christ, nevertheless I live, yet not I, but Christ Who lives in me." God is anxious to pour out His grace to enable us to live out the Christian life each moment of each day, as we recognize the Source of that blessing. We must consciously make the decision to put this principle into our daily living, and having done so, this principle is true no matter what life brings to us. As we live this kind of "exchanged life," God is prepared to walk with us and help us in every decision we make in life.

The apostle Paul states this principle a little differently in 1 Corinthians 15;10, "But by the grace of God, I am what I am, and His grace toward me was not in vein." In this verse the apostle is undoubtedly referring mainly to the fact that he was saved by the grace of God, and he ministers to the Lord by His grace. But it is also true that in every phase of his life, he rejoices in the grace of God at work in him. This would include his entire experience of life including the trials and sufferings he endured (2 Cor. 11:22-33). He could not have made it without grace. Beyond the truth of grace in salvation and sanctification is the fact of grace at work in the daily Christian life of the believer as he/she faces circumstances, trials, sickness, disappointment, discouragement, as well as the unknowns in life.

Paul learned this lesson as he faced a physical disability. He pleaded with God to remove the infirmity that was plaguing him. God answered him with the word that His grace was to replace the healing that Paul desired. That grace was sufficient to meet his need and give him the victory he needed for living (2 Cor. 12: 9, 10). Notice Paul's response in a two-fold joyful assurance; he is glad to continue living with the infirmity and even to be proud of having it, and he also recognizes that with the infirmity the power of Christ rests on him. The word he uses for rest is the same word that is used for Christ in John 1:14 which says that the Lord dwelt, or literally tabernacled among us. The power of Christ tabernacled or rested on Paul's life. That power was an evident part of his being, such that he was content to live with his physical problem. It is amazing to think that a person would believe that God's power in a life is more enjoyable than being free from bodily infirmity. What person in his right mind would be glad to carry an infirmity, unless God's grace is so evident that the person knows that God is involved with his pain? This was Paul's attitude toward his trial. He knew that God was intimately involved in his life, and that was enough to make him content with his physical problem. He chose grace over comfort, not an easy choice.

There are many people who live in constant pain and physical affliction. Suffering is a fact of life. To some, it comes sooner than expected, to some it comes later, especially as older people face their infirmities. But like Paul, they need to depend daily on the grace of God to get them through life. God is there to supply what they need. But what if we become discouraged with life? What if we think that His grace is not sufficient? Does that mean that we have given up on His grace? No, it means that we have forgotten God's promise to supply that need. If He says "My grace is sufficient", who are we to say, "No God, it isn't sufficient?" We have every right before God to put Him to the test and claim that He must supply the grace He has promised. And we believe that is exactly what He wants us to do. We are to lay hold of His promise, and many other promises for each occasion. We do have anxieties and fears. We do have uncertainties. And for each situation, God has a promise of His grace to see us through. We make the conscious decision to allow that to happen.

2. GRACE AND DAILY PROVISIONS

Another aspect of grace in daily living is the daily provisions of God for our lives The word grace is not found in the Bible in conjunction with the exodus journeys of the children in the wilderness. But who can doubt that the Lord showed His grace to the Israelites when He faithfully provided manna to sustain them, along with clothing and shoes that did not wear out during the years of wandering (Deut. 29:5). Not only was it grace, but it would seem to have been miraculous to wear sandals or shoes forty years without getting a hole in them, or having them wear out. God's promise to provide for His children certainly proved true in this instance.

When we pray the Lord's prayer, we make the request "give us this day our daily bread." The Lord does that consistently, as he did to the children in the wilderness. But we do not always think of it as God's grace to us, but rather our own efforts or work that has provided our daily provisions. However, we can take a principle of God's provision from Paul in 1 Corinthians 3:6-7, "I planted, Apollos watered, but God gave the increase. So then neither he who plants is anything, nor he who waters, but God who gives the increase." Paul applied this principle in winning people to Christ. He said that some lay the groundwork in witnessing, others follow up and possibly lead the person to the Lord, but it is God who does the actual regenerating of a soul. In comparison, this quotation can also be applied to the physical provisions of life. If it wasn't for God's grace to allow a harvest of crops, all of the efforts of people in planting the seed and watering the ground would be useless. If it wasn't for the daily provisions that God's kindness provides to a family, all of the efforts to work or labor would be in vain.

Referring to Paul again, we see that he did not know where his sustenance in life would come from. Yes, he worked as a tent maker, but also was dependent on God's people to meet his needs. Paul says in Philippians 4:16-17 that the Philippian Church provided for him. He did not ask for that, but they were used of God to meet his needs. He calls the material goods given by others a gift from God given through the church as a sacrifice which pleases God. God is the Provider, the church is the avenue of supply, and God gets the glory for what He has provided. It's all about God, and all about grace!

Another illustration of this principle of God's daily provision can be taken from the Sermon on the Mount. Some think of the Sermon on the Mount as an example of the modus operandi of God during the kingdom age. Others with a different hermeneutical viewpoint believe that these principles are for us today. No matter where you come down theologically, the principle of God's provision is the point to be made in Matthew 6:25-34. God is the Provider of food and clothing. Jesus says this in light of man's natural concerns to provide for his family, or for himself physically. Four times He uses the expression "take no thought", or as another version says, "do not worry." Jesus says this in regard to our life (V. 25), our physical stature (V. 27), our clothing

(V. 28), and our food and drink (V. 30). Jesus emphasizes that the animal kingdom does not fret about their provisions to sustain life, because God is their supplier. He graciously gives them what they need. The Lord chides His listeners by telling them not to worry because God knows their needs. And if He knows the needs, will He not graciously supply them apart from what people can do? Our responsibility is to be more concerned about our spiritual condition than our material condition.

This is not an excuse to be lazy or sit back and wait for God to drop the food and clothes from heaven into our laps similarly to what He did in providing manna in the wilderness for the Israelites. Other passages state that we are to labor honestly to provide for ourselves and our family (Gen. 1:28; Eph. 4: 28; 2 Thess. 3:12). The book of Proverbs has a lot to say about laziness and provisions. Jesus is making the point in His sermon that God is the Source of all our necessities in life. We are to receive these gifts with thanksgiving especially as we bow our heads and say "grace" before meals; an interesting expression to use but very accurate when we think of the grace of God in supplying our needs.

Another example of God's provision of grace in our daily living as believers is the grace of forgiveness. We discussed this topic above as a principle or method in which God's deals with us. We view it now as a furnishing of His grace in our lives in relation to others. This may be one of the hardest aspects of Christian living in allowing God's grace to so work in us that we are joyful in forgiving another person. Our natural tendency toward those who wrong us is to get back at or get even with them. This is not the Christ-like way to handle life's conflicts with others.

King David is probably one of the best examples of the grace of God working in his life to forgive another person. King Saul learned to hate David, and was deeply jealous of his successes, fearful that someday David would become king instead of Saul's son Jonathan. Saul tried on more than one occasion to kill David. David was forced to flee for his life from Saul. On two occasions David had the opportunity to kill Saul in revenge (1 Sam. Chapters 24 & 26). However, on each occasion David withheld vengeance, believing that someday God would honor David's patience and settle the account justly. John Piper would call this living by faith in future grace, by which in overcoming vengeance and bitterness, a person trusts God to deal justly with the affairs of his life. (Piper 1995, 261). Later, when David learned of Saul's death in battle along with his son Jonathan, David mourned for them both and honored Saul in his lamentation as well as his beloved friend Jonathan (2 Sam. Chapter 1). Only the grace of God at work in David could have allowed him to show such kindness toward a person who was filled with hatred toward him.

The book of Genesis has a large section that tells the story of Joseph, one of the twelve sons of Jacob. Joseph was mistreated, mocked, and hated by his brothers. Approximately twenty years later and after a number of trials in his life, Joseph meets his brothers again. Through a series of tests that he puts to his brothers, Joseph learns that they are now sorry for the way they treated him. Joseph weeps at their change of heart and forgives them (Gen.45:2,15). God was at work in Joseph to show kindness and grace toward his brothers rather than trying to get even for what they did to him. In each of these two stories, the word grace is not used, but the evidence of grace is seen in the lives of both David and Joseph.

It is said of Jesus in John 1:14 that He was "full of grace and truth." Nowhere is this grace more evident than when He hung on the cross and cried out to the Father to forgive those who hung Him there (Luke 23:34). Paul reminds us in Ephesians 4:32 to "Forgive one another, as Christ also has forgiven us." And how did Jesus do that? Through the abundant grace of God flowing in His life. God also provides the grace in our lives to do the same. In fact that is the only way that we can forgive. John 1:16 shows us that truth. The evangelist says that we have received grace upon grace from the fullness of Christ's grace. As the Lord was able by grace to forgive His enemies, so also the believer is able to do the same. Apart from that grace of Christ working within the believer, forgiveness to another person is impossible. In summary, we see that the grace of God is the method and means for the Christian to live after he has been sovereignly chosen by God to become His child.

J.C. Ryle sums up the topic of God's grace in daily living and provisions very succinctly as he quotes from David in Ps. 37:25 "I have been young, and now am old; yet I have not seen the righteous forsaken, not His descendants begging bread." (Ryle 2007, 61). God is the gracious Provider of daily needs, whether it is the need for the material things of life, or the spiritual need to live the Christian life.

3. GRACE AND DYING

It is often said that God does not give us grace that we do not need, but when the occasion arises, He will provide the grace to see us through the situation. Such is the case when we face dying. This is life's most challenging trial that we face. If we ever needed grace to see us through that crisis, that is the time to experience it. There are no direct Bible passages that tell us that God provides grace when we are dying. Paul tells us that death has lost its sting because of the resurrection of Christ (1Cor. 15:54, 55). Believers need never fear death when they face that hour. The only passages we can examine on this topic are the examples of believers facing death.

There are a number of stories that we can refer to. Three examples will suffice. Perhaps the most dramatic and miraculous illustration is the story of the three Hebrews in the fiery furnace (Dan. Ch. 3). Shadrach, Meshach, and Abednego defied King Nebuchadnezzar's order to bow down and worship the idol that the king had built. They were ordered to be thrown into the fiery furnace, but were given one last chance to recant. They held firm to their conviction of worshipping only Jehovah. But before being cast into the furnace, the men made a dramatic confession of their faith, *O Nebuchadnezzar, we have no need to answer you in this matter. If that is the case, our God whom we serve is able to deliver us from the burning fiery furnace, and He will deliver us from your hand, O King. But if not, let it be known to you, O King, that we do not serve your gods, not will we worship the gold image which you have set up (Dan. 3:16-18)*

The three men believed that God could save them from physical death, and so defy the flames. But they also included the thought that if God was not pleased to deliver them, they would face their fate and be faithful to God no matter what the outcome might be. This is a story of the faith of these men, but it is also a story of the grace of God poured out in their lives for them to believe that they could face death victoriously and unafraid.

God miraculously delivers the three men from the flames. But there is a dramatic event in the story that tempers the threat of death which can be applicable to every believer. In the midst of the flames there is a fourth person standing there with them. Nebuchadnezzar sees this person and exclaims "The form of the fourth is like the son of the gods" (Dan. 3:25). This is how the Chaldeans interpreted the miracle of the fourth person. We are not sure whether this fourth person is a divine appearance of Christ, or of an angel. In any case, God placed a fourth person to stand with the men to face this fiery trial. The king calls for the men to come out of the furnace since they were not killed. The story relates the fact that the clothes of the three men were not burned, nor was their hair singed by the flames. However, the cords that bound them were destroyed. Is that not strange that some earthly things were consumed (ropes), but others not consumed (hair, clothes)? Not only does God give us grace to face death, but in the actual trial He is there to stand with us and guide us through the event, bringing us safely to the other side in heaven. In this story God did deliver the three Hebrews from death. In other situations He may not allow that. Many martyrs for Christ have suffered death. The lesson for us is that God is with those who face this situation.

In Acts chapter seven Stephan is another example of the grace of God in facing death. This is the Biblical example of thousands who have died in martyrdom, and are still dying today. After his strong defense of the Gospel and testimony to the Jews, the crowd begins to stone Stephan. This was the Jewish way of killing a supposed blasphemer. Before he closes his eyes in death, Stephan sees heaven open and the Lord Jesus standing at the right hand of God (Acts. 7:55). Scripture tells us that Jesus is seated at the Father's right hand

and is interceding for believers (Col. 3:1; Heb. 7:25; 1 John 2:1; etc.). Jesus' standing at Stephan's martyrdom seems to indicate that He honors Stephan as He welcomes him home to glory. The God of grace shows that grace to Stephan in allowing him to see the presence of the Lord at death. We cannot say that the Lord always stands in honor of those who give themselves as martyrs for His name. Nor can we say that He does this with other Christians who die. But we can conjecture that God provides some form of His grace to ease the uncertainty of death in the life of a believer, whether it is in the assurance of His presence, the sight of heaven, the voice of God calling the believer home, or the calm assurance that God gives the person in this time of crisis.

Paul is the third example of this form of God's grace in the life of a believer preparing to die. The apostle writes in Philippians 1:21 "To me to live is Christ, and to die is gain." For Paul death was welcomed. A person cannot have that realization unless there is the calmness of God in his soul. Paul states further in Philippians 1:23 that to depart this life is far better than living. It is true that Paul did have a glimpse of heaven in a previous encounter with the spiritual world (2 Cor. 12:4) and this would have prepared him to have a greater desire for heaven. But having said that, the actual departure from this life is not lessened in frightfulness because the transition from life to death still must take place and is an unknown mystery. Paul answers that struggle also in 2 Timothy 4: 6-7. He has done all that God wanted him to do in life, and now he awaits death at the hands of Emperor Nero in a Roman jail. What does the apostle say? His life is to be poured out as a libation for God. There is no fear in his ultimate fate at the hands of the executioner. Paul has the calmness of God in his breast, placed there by the grace of God

4. CONCLUDING THOUGHTS ON GRACE

Someone has said of believers, "we are not living people waiting to die, but dying people waiting to live." While we live in these bodies, we live by God's abundant never ending grace in our lives. That grace may be described as the benevolent kindness of the Lord to His creatures. In all of the sections above, we should note that grace is not something of an abstract element, but a living and active manifestation of a part of God's character that is revealed in acts of kindness which He performs in our lives. He works sanctification to make us like Christ. He performs in our lives when we go through trials, or when we are tempted by Satan. He acts in grace in forgiving us when we sin. God gives us an assurance of His presence in our dying moments. He does all this through grace. It is God Himself Who works to make the Christian life a reality. That is why the statement "God's modus operandi in the believer's life is grace" becomes the foundation of God's dealings with His children. The Holy Spirit enacts what God has placed in our lives to make it a sovereign act, and none of our doing. The *International Standard Bible Encyclopedia* suggests that the word grace is almost a synonym for the Holy Spirit, *Evidently in this sense "grace" is almost a synonym for the Spirit, and there is little real difference between "full of the Holy Spirit," and "full of grace and power," in Acts 6:5,8 while there is a very striking parallel between Eph. 4:7-13 and 1 Cor. 12:4-11, with "gifts of grace" in the one passage and "gifts of the Spirit" in the other. And this connection between grace and the Spirit is found definitely in the formula "Spirit of grace" in Heb. 10:29 (Orr Vol. II 1930, 1290-91)*

This indeed makes grace the unmerited favor of the Lord to us. John 1:16 says that we have received of Christ's fullness His "grace for grace." This prepositional phrase can be translated "grace upon grace." One blessing upon another is continually heaped upon us throughout our Christian lives. It never ends! The Greek word *anti*, which means "in place of" is used for the preposition in that phrase. Robertson in his *Word Pictures in the New Testament* describes it as one grace taking the place of another grace each day, similarly to the Israelite children in the wilderness when they received fresh manna from heaven each day. The new day's supply replaced the previous day's quantity. Just as the manna was never exhausted until the children of Israel reached the Promised Land, so the grace of God in our lives is never ending, but is renewed daily to enable us to live according to the plan that God has for our lives until we reach glory.

Grace is not only inexhaustible in supply, but it is given in fullness. Vincent in his *Word Studies in the New Testament* defines the word *fullness* as complete in itself or an entire quantity (Vincent Vol. II 2009, 37). Since grace is given in fullness as well as in continuous measure, we cannot humanly comprehend the extent of the riches of God's grace poured out on us. An infinite supply, infinitely and continuously given to us. That takes the breathe away! The *International Standard Bible Encyclopedia* says that, "grace...is an attitude on God's part that proceeds entirely from within Himself, and that is conditioned in no way by anything in the objects of His favor." (Orr Vol. II 1930, 1291). Along with being inexhaustible and continuous, the grace of God is freely given from the intent of God's heart alone to meet the need of every season of life, and every situation that we face as long as we live. We close this section with the words written by Graham Kendrick in his song, *Only By Grace*, which expresses so effectively the truth of this topic, ***Only by grace can we enter, only by grace can*** *we stand, Not by our human endeavor, but by the blood of the Lamb. Into your presence You call us, You call us to come Into your presence you draw and now by your grace we come. Lord if you mark our transgressions, who would stand? Thanks to your grace we are cleansed by the blood of the Lamb.*

PART 3 - THE GLORY OF GOD

CHAPTER 9
GLORY - THE MAGNIFICANCE OF GOD IN ALL THINGS

1. THE DEFINITION OF GOD'S GLORY

In dealing with this topic, I feel overwhelmed, and sometimes think that I have gotten into something to deep that I cannot even realize or conceptualize. How can any human being grasp the truth of the glory of God? Impossible, but we try anyway! There are two approaches to defining the word. One is to view the concept from the aspect of what a person does, i.e. ascribe praise, honor or adoration to something or someone that to an individual seems beyond the ordinary. He might say, "That is a glorious sight" (we would use the word "awesome" today). The other aspect of the thought is to view the word from the giver of that glory. For example the pageantry of a royal wedding would show the glory of the royal family and the majesty of the event. This would evoke praise from the viewer.

We want to especially notice the second aspect of the word. Therefore, one definition of glory is, "That which displays the excellence of the subject." This fits the descriptions of God when we read about His glory in Scripture. The meaning of the Old Testament word kabod is glory, and refers to God in His manifestation, dignity, or preeminence, such as the manifestation of the Shekinah glory that was over the Tabernacle, or that light which guided the children of Israel in the wilderness. Solomon also saw the glory of God as he dedicated the temple causing the children of Israel to say in worship, "For He is good, and His mercy endures forever." (2 Chronicles 7:2) This is the same word used in Psalm 19:1, "The heavens declare the glory of God, and the firmament shows His handiwork." Glory is the form in which God chooses to reveal Himself to His creation and creatures.

The word for glory in the New Testament is doxa. Colin Brown, in his *Dictionary of New Testament Theology* defines the word as, "Always something given to God or one's fellow man...but in the Bible it is a quality belonging to God and is recognized by man only in response to Him." (Brown Vol. II 1981, 44). From this thought we see that the glory of God is in the world and has nothing to do with man's ability to increase or decrease that attribute. However, only when man is in tune with God will that glory be realized or confessed in the way God wants us to understand that attribute. That is because only the regenerate person can truly recognize God and the work He is performing both in the heart and in the world.

2. GOD JEALOUSLY GUARDS HIS GLORY

To talk about the jealousy of God is just as strange to us as saying that God seeks mankind to praise Him for His glory. But this topic of God's jealousy is related closely to the glory of God. The word jealousy definitely has a negative connotation in our vocabulary, and a sinful connotation in our society. But jealousy can have a positive connotation also, and this is the way in which it is used of God. As an illustration, a husband and wife are happily married. They are jealous for the love of each other and for no one else. They want no other person to come between that relationship. Paul uses this concept in 2 Corinthians 11:2 when he says, "I am jealous over you with godly jealousy, for I have espoused you to one husband, that I may present you a chaste virgin to Christ." Paul wants no other love to come between the church of Corinth and God. Tragically, that was not the case in the Corinthian Church. There was much sin in the fellowship, and the believers had two spiritual lovers; God and the world. This hurt Paul deeply and he wrote two letters to the Corinthian Church to correct this adulterous spiritual perversion. This is exactly the way God feels in His relationship with humankind. He wants all of His creation to love Him alone. Satan wants to steal that love of God from believers, and to come between the Lord and people. When that happens, God reacts jealously toward His creation. His response is found in Exodus 20:3-6 as part of His Ten Commandments, a portion of which says, *You shall have no other gods before Me. You shall not make for yourselves a carved image - any likeness of anything that is in heaven above, or that is in the earth beneath, or that is in the water under the earth: you shall not bow down to them or serve them, for I, the Lord your God, am a JEALOUS GOD (capitals mine).* The Lord refers here to a carved image or what we call an idol. A broader concept of the word idol would be anything that takes the place of God as a priority in life. It need not be a carved image. God wants all of us, and nothing must come between us and Him.

The prophet Isaiah picks up this theme in Isaiah 42:8, "I am the Lord, that is My name: and My glory I will not give to another, nor My praise to carved images." Jehovah is His name, which means the self- existing One. Nothing exists apart from Him. Thus He is worthy to be the highest consideration of man's thoughts. His glory is to be the highest attainment that man can achieve in honoring the self-existing One.

There are at least ten references in the Bible which directly refer to God being jealous, and other verses which imply that truth. All of the references are in the Old Testament. Most of the passages are related to Israel's departure from God. There are no New Testament scriptures that use the phrase "jealous God." The Lord looked on Israel as His bride. But sin caused her to depart from Him. In His jealous desire to repair that relationship, God both punishes and then attempts to restore the Israelites to Him. Unfortunately, full restoration will not occur until the final day when God's glory will be seen by the nation of Israel and they will fully recognize that His jealous love wins out.

We generally think of the glory of God in relation to the end of the world when He shall reign over all creation, and will receive the honor and praise that He deserves. But that glory of God is seen also in all of His manifested and manifold perfections, not only at the end of the ages. For example, creation itself shows His glory. Psalm 19:1 was quoted above. When He is merciful, His glory is seen. When He is gracious, that expresses His glory. When He is loving and redemptive to His sinful creation, that is a manifestation of His glory. Yes, even when the world seems to be spinning out of control, or when our world is in chaos, His glory is mysteriously being manifested in ways that we do not understand. In revealing these aspects of God's glory, He also manifests His jealousy since He wants all humankind to acknowledge His attributes and involvement in order to give Him the glory alone. When man does not do this, He becomes jealous.

In considering the sovereignty of God, and His purposes for the world, we note from Scripture that the flow of history is lineal. That is, God has an end purpose for the culmination of the events He sovereignly has designed. But He also has an end game for the everyday events of humankind which is to magnify Himself and His glory. When God pours out His grace in immeasurable ways, He again has an end game to reveal His glory and extreme generosity to His creation. This body of truth is perhaps the most precious of all the thoughts we can have of a loving God. Because of His perfections, He can desire that all creation, humankind, and events in the world bring honor to Him. From a human standpoint this seems unreal. We would say that this is the ultimate of selfishness. Why should God want to receive so much attention to Himself such that not only creation praises Him, but He also does not want anyone else to be praised above Him? The answer is found in part when we take a frail human illustration, and attempt to compare that to an infinite God.

We honor the memory of George Washington, Abraham Lincoln, Ronald Reagan or even a great athlete for their great accomplishments in their fields of expertise. Their names are revered, we make statutes of those people. Buildings, roads, bridges, and parks are named in their honor. They are esteemed for their accomplishments. Now take this same principle and apply it to God Almighty. No one has accomplished as much as God. No name is to be honored more highly than His. All creation bows before Him for the greatest of His sovereign plans, especially His marvelous design of salvation. Who is worthy of more honor than He? In all honesty, God is pleased with this recognition and finds ultimate joy when His creatures also recognize the results of His work. He finds pleasure and satisfaction in Himself when He realizes that all He has done magnifies Himself in magnifying His accomplishments. His magnificence and glory are shared with His creatures. John Piper is well known for his statement, "God is most glorified in us when we are most satisfied with Him" (Piper 1995, 9). God's honor is uplifted, and we are the beneficiaries resulting in our own joy in being the children of God.

There are some Scripture passages that might be construed as saying that God seeks glory. This can be interpreted to mean that He wants to enhance His glory that He gains from humanity. This is not accurate. God has never been less than glorious, nor has He ever lacked glory that needed to be increased by humanity's praise of Him. Since God is self-contained, His glory is also a part of that self-containment. The scriptures say that the glory He possesses is enhanced by the way He acts, or in the way that man ascribes honor to Him. But that does not increase His glory. One cannot increase infinity and God is infinitely glorious! By the same token, when humankind does not glorify God by his actions, this does not lessen God's glory since He is infinite. God wants to receive glory from his creation in recognition of what He has done for humankind. It is to our benefit that we give honor to or recognize God's glory. It is not for His benefit. When we pray that God may be glorified, we are not asking God to increase His glory, but to display that infinite glory which He already possesses in that particular situation.

3. THE GLORY OF GOD IN THE BOOK OF EPHESIANS

The foundation of this book is taken from Ephesians 1:3-14. In the bigger picture, the word *glory* is found eight times in Ephesians; three of which are found in this section. Ephesians 1:6 says, "To the praise of the glory of His grace by which He made us accepted in the beloved." Ephesians 1:12 states, "That we, who first trusted in Christ should be to the praise of His glory." Finally, Ephesians 1:14 says, "Who is the guarantee of our inheritance until the redemption of the purchased possession to the praise of His glory." Of the other five statements mentioning the word glory, four of them refer to God's glory.

The context of the word glory in Ephesians 1:6 is that saints have been predestined from the foundation of the world, and have been adopted into Christ's family. We have seen from verse 6 that the sovereignty of God is manifested in His grace. Now we see the role that glory plays in this triumvirate of sovereignty, grace, and glory. Glory displays itself in showing God's grace. The phrase in Ephesians 1:6 may well be translated, "To His glorious grace." Paul is saying that we are to admire the sovereignty and grace of God through the glory which we ascribe to Him. That glory which was always His is shown in the marvelous work of redemption. One commentator has said that the glory of God is the supreme end of all that he does. What God has done for mankind in His plan of salvation can only well up in the hearts of believers as an expression of adoration and the giving of glory to God.

In Ephesians 1:6, the view of giving glory to God is seen from the aspect of eternity. It appears that Paul is saying that we should do this now as believers who have trusted in Christ in light of what we will do in eternity. Verse 12 may refer to Jews, since verse 13 uses the word "you," probably referring to Gentiles. Both Jews and Gentiles are to give glory to God because of what they have received in Christ. In the wider context of the epistle, it is the Church of Christ to whom Paul refers to. In giving glory to God, Paul is saying that we have no reason to boast about what has been graced to us. It is all about God and His glory.

Finally in our seminal passage, Ephesians 1:14 introduces the Holy Spirit as part of the plan of salvation. He seals the believer until the day of final redemption. This shows the work of the Trinity in the overall plan of salvation. To summarize this jubilant adoration, the glory of the Father is seen in the choosing and election of the saints, the glory of the Son is seen in His work of redemption and the inheritance we have in Christ, and the glory of the Holy Spirit is seen in His sealing and preservation of the saints. It is indeed all about God's glory! Ephesians 1:17-18 states, *That the God of our Lord Jesus Christ, the Father of glory, may give to you the Spirit of wisdom and revelation in the knowledge of Him, the eyes of your understanding being enlightened; that you may know what is the hope of His calling, what are the riches of the glory of His inheritance in the saints.*

In Ephesians 3:16 we read, "That he would grant you according to the riches of His glory to be strengthened with might through His Spirit in the inner man." From this brief survey of these verses we note that the Father is praised for His glory which is very rich, His grace which is glorious, and the inheritance of believers which also is glorious. Paul is stating what we have concluded above; the glory of God is the essence of His nature, and is the sum of all the beautiful things He does, whether it is the design of His plan of salvation, or the effect of that plan resulting in the Church of Christ which is to the praise of his glory.

Finally in Ephesians 3:21 Paul says, "To Him be glory in the Church by Christ Jesus to all generations, forever and ever, Amen." God's glory is seen in this Church Age by the magnificence of His work in the universal body of believers in Christ. The author of Ephesians refers to this concept vividly in an extended explanation in two other passages of the book. Chapter two reveals that there is no distinction between Jew and Gentile. Both are one in Christ because of His work uniting all mankind in the Body of Christ. Chapter three makes reference to the oneness of all believers. Paul was privileged to reveal this truth to the church at Ephesus, and to believers in general. In Ephesians 3:10, Paul says that God is so pleased to make known this manifold wisdom of the creation of the Body of Christ, He uses the Church to display that wisdom to the "principalities and powers in the heavenly places," probably referring to the fallen creatures.

4. THE GLORY OF GOD IN ELECTION

We have seen the glory of God in the book of Ephesians, and the manner in which Paul uses that phrase. We also looked at the sovereignty of God in choosing us. Now we want to go into more detail and tie together the sovereignty of God with His glory. We begin with the passages which show that God's choosing was for His own glory and purposes. One of the most prominent verses which declares His election of believers is found in John 6:44, "No one can come to me unless the Father who sent me draws him; and I will raise him up on the last day." Jesus enhances that truth in John 15:16, "You did not choose me, but I chose you, and appointed you that you should go and bear fruit, and that your fruit should remain." Note that the Savior says these words making Him co-equal with the Father in the plan of election. Because people do not have the power or ability to choose themselves to become citizens of the kingdom of God, the Lord Himself must choose. Indeed, because they are sinners, they will not naturally want to choose the salvation that God offers them because they must humble themselves to receive the gift of salvation, a position that no sinner wants to accept. God must draw the chosen ones to open their hearts to the wooing of the Spirit. Herein lies the first aspect of His glory in election. Since He makes the final call as to who will be redeemed, He does this to enhance His marvelous plan.

There are some who believe that because of the omniscience of God, He can look into the future and see who will receive Him as Savior. God then prepares the circumstances or the right people to enter the life of the unsaved and causes them to respond to the grace of God. But in saying this we diminish the glory of God and the method of His election. As stated above, we are incapable of choosing Him. There is a cogent statement that summarizes this thought. The statement says that God did not see Saul the persecutor one day becoming Paul the great apostle and soul winner, and so arranged for his salvation on the road to Damascus. Rather, God chose Saul for His own glory before the foundation of the world in order to make Paul the great apostle and soul winner. God did arrange the circumstances for Saul's conversion, but only after He had sovereignly ordained the election of Saul before time began. If God did not choose Saul to become a believer, then Saul would never have become Paul. That lays the salvation and the glory of that action squarely in the hands of God.

The second aspect of this glorious election is found in the truth of John 6:37, "All that the Father gives me will come to me, and the one who comes to me I will by no means cast out ." The choosing of our salvation is in the hands of God. When He makes that decision as to who the person(s) is, the election is sure and secure. Again this enhances His glory as to the truthfulness of His person and character. When He makes a statement, we can be sure that the truth of that statement will never change. We come to the Father because He draws us with the delight of the offer of His salvation that we cannot refuse. A simple illustration will help us. If we place a magnet in a field of materials such as nails, aluminum, and wood, the only item that will be attracted to the magnet is the iron. The iron cannot do anything else but be drawn to the magnet because it "delights" so to speak in the magnet and is capable of being attracted to it. Aluminum and wood are incapable of being drawn to a magnet so they stay where they are placed. In being drawn to the magnet the iron cannot escape its attraction and will permanently be attached to the magnet as long as the magnet retains its electrical charge to draw metal. The Lord has attracted us by the drawing of His Spirit to the person and work of Christ. The Spirit's ministry is so beautiful and satisfying that when God opens the spiritual eyes of our hearts, we cannot refuse to come to Him even though we may not understand all of its implications or the theology behind our decision. The result is that the Lord's all powerful "magnetic" drawing will never let go of the person whom He has attracted to the Savior. The original Greek for the expression "by no means" in John 6:37 is a double negative for emphasis, and may be translated "never, never." The Lord is saying that we are eternally secure, and He will never, never let us go. His power to hold us is eternal and omnipotent.

CHAPTER 10
ILLUSTRATIONS OF THE
GLORY OF GOD

1. THE ANGELS GIVE GLORY TO GOD

This is not a study in angelology, but a study in creation giving glory to God. Before man was created, God created angels who were with Him in heaven. Although God has given some of them other assignments, such as serving humankind as His divine messenger i.e. appearances to Abraham and others, the birth of Jesus, or ministering to believers (Hebrews 1:14), their principle function seems to be worshipping God. In Job 38:7, God questions Job as to where Job was when the earth was formed. He says, "When the morning stars sang together, and all the sons of God shouted for joy." The verse makes mention of the angels as "morning stars." But in Hebrew parallelism when a phrase is repeated, God calls the angels "sons of God", not because they are what we would call believers or born again children of God, but because they are the creation of God. At that time, the angels shouted for joy at the handiwork of the Lord laying the foundation of the earth. The shout was so loud that it split the ears. That is the meaning of the Hebrew word *shout* in this context. They saw what the hand of the Lord did and they gave glory to Him because of His mighty power.

In another passage, it appears from Ezekiel chapter 28 that Lucifer (who later is infamously named Satan) was the leader of the host of angels. He directed the choir of angels in worshipping and praising God before man was created. Myriads of angels, or thousands of them, were created for this purpose. Psalm 68:17 talks about thousands and thousands of angels. Hebrews 12:22 expresses the number as an innumerable company of angelic beings. Nehemiah 9:6 reminds us in his prayer that the host of heaven worship God. The angels are exhorted in Psalm 148:2 to praise the Lord. Revelation 7:11 tells us that angels stand around the throne of God to offer worship to Him. Since this is a picture of heaven, we conclude that this worship of God has been occurring since these beings were created. It seems logical to suppose that these creatures were made to perform acts of adoration to God and to give Him glory.

One of the most powerful examples of angels giving glory to God is found in Isaiah 6:2. The prophet sees a vision of the Lord's throne with *seraphim* surrounding the throne of the Lord. These celestial beings are a superior order of angels that we read about in scripture, and attend to God's throne. The word seraphim is derived from the meaning which signifies "burning" or "burning ones." This is consistent with verse six which states that one of the seraphim took coals of fire from the altar to touch Isaiah's lips. The word seraphim is in the plural telling us that there is more than one seraph performing this service of worship. Isaiah 6:3 states, "And one cried to another and said: holy, holy, holy is the Lord of hosts; the whole earth is full of His glory." We can also translate this last phase as "the whole earth is the fullness of His glory." Everything that God created on earth is an expression of His glory, and the seraphim recognize and confess this truth. Even in a sin cursed world, God's glory shines through.

We do not read much about the fall of angels. 2 Peter 2:4 indicates that God cast out of heaven the angels that rebelled with Satan. Some were chained and others are presently free to roam about in the earth. We contend with these angels (demons) when we wage spiritual warfare, fighting against the "principalities, powers, and rulers of the darkness of this age, and spiritual hosts of wickedness in heavenly places" (Eph. 6:12). But even these fallen angels are subject to giving glory to God. That truth is found in Mark chapter 5 in the story of the demoniac at Gadera with the legion of demons indwelling the demon possessed man. When Jesus released the man from his condition, the demons asked Jesus not to send them to Hades, but to allow them to enter the swine. Jesus had the power to do that, showing the exercise of His right to control fallen angels, and their subjection to His authority and glory.

Philippians 2:10 says that every knee will bow to the name of Jesus, whether it is those in heaven, on earth, or under the earth. This wide category of all creation includes the fallen angels. Although they are condemned to hell, they will also acknowledge the glory of God. The angels referred to above who are chained would also be in the class of those "under the earth" who will express their submission to God and give Him glory.

2. CREATION TELLS OF THE GLORY OF GOD

Just as we gave examples of the sovereignty of God in chapter 3, so we want to give illustrations of His glory as we observe it in the created world. The first illustration, and perhaps the easiest way to show this truth is in the Scriptures which talk about His glory as displayed in creation. Two obvious passages come to mind immediately: Psalm 8:1,3 and Psalm 19:1. In the latter passage, David looked up into the night sky and was able to see with his naked eye about 5000 stars differing in brilliance, color, and in varying constellations. His reaction was to realize the power, greatness, and majesty of God in such a sight. With today's instruments and especially the Hubble Telescope, we see billions of stars, constellations, and heavenly phenomena that were unexplainable in David's day. The stars are placed in the firmament, but the expanse of the sky is trillions of light years across. Scientists tell us that this universe is expanding to even larger proportions. That is mind boggling! How can a firmament (that which is firm) be moving? This majestic sight enhances and magnifies David's statement in scripture regarding the glory of God.

That glory is also seen in the way God causes these heavenly phenomena to move consistently and faithfully through the skies day after day, year after year, and millennia after millennia. We are able to predict the date when a comet, such as Halley's Comet, will appear scores of years before the event happens. We can predict the occurrence of sun and moon eclipses, and when stars will be in conjunction. This shows the orderliness and dependability of the Creator, another aspect which enhances His glory.

Our immediate eye sees the sun and moon. The glory of the sun is seen in its brilliance to light and heat the earth. If it is too close, we would burn up. If it is too far away, we would freeze. God designed the earth and sun to be in the right proportion of distance to each other to allow us to live here on earth. That brings Him glory. David was never able to see or comprehend this as we do today, but through faith his imagination could picture the greatness of God's glory in designing such a universe.

We come back again to Psalm 19:1 which mentions the "handiwork of God," and tie that with Psalm 8:3 which talks of "the work of Your fingers." We think of God speaking and by His power things are or will be created. These two verses seem to indicate that God actually designed with His fingers (can a Spirit have fingers?) the moon and the stars. His hand moves, or perhaps He speaks and a star multi thousands of times the size of the earth is created. There are multi millions of those stars! God is powerful enough to simply think creation, and it will happen. But it is a beautiful thought to realize that God is an Artist who personally takes an interest in His creation, shaping each star with its own size and brilliance, calling each one by its own name (Ps. 147:4). God is not Someone afar off who designs a universe and then leaves it spinning in space. He is a personal God even to His inanimate creation. Furthermore, it appears that the inanimate creation responds to the Creator's act by declaring His glory. Psalm 65:8 indicates that the sun in the morning, and the moon in the evening appear to rejoice and give pleasure in doing what they do, i.e. give light and heat to the earth. And they do this as long as God continues to direct their activities. Psalm 148:3-4 states, "Praise Him, sun and moon; praise Him all you stars of light! Praise Him you heavens of heavens." Can you picture the glories of heaven with all of their praise as these objects fulfill their purpose in ascribing glory to God? It must be unbelievably rapturous.

From the mightiest creation of the stars and the universe, we also see the glory of God in the multitude of various small creations, some so small that they cannot be seen with the naked eye, yet each with unique design. Microscopes and electron accelerators are needed to study this design and motion to realize that this phenomena awes the mind. Another facet of His glory can be seen if a person goes to the aquarium and study's the creatures that live in the depths of the sea. They reveal the handiwork of God. Some of these sea urchins never see the light of day, and live hundreds of miles below sea level. Yet, they are there by His design, and God receives as much joy and glory in seeing these animals swim the depths of the ocean unseen by human eyes as when He flings the stars in space which are also unseen by the human eye. Psalm 148:7 states, "Praise the Lord from the earth, you great sea creatures and all the depths." And God adds His own commentary in Genesis chapter one when He continually says of His creation, "God saw that it was good."

But these wonders of creation are all eclipsed by the wonder of the human being, that God said is made in His image. A tiny male sperm and female egg that need to be examined under a microscope are joined together mysteriously to form a person. God marvelously breaths into that union the breath of life. After only a few weeks, the parts of the body are discernible. David sums it up beautifully when He says in Psalm 139:13-16, *For You formed my inward parts; You covered me in my mother's womb. I will praise you for I am fearfully and wonderfully made; marvelous are Your works, and that my soul knows very well. My frame was not hidden from You when I was made in secret, and skillfully wrought in the lowest parts of the earth. Your eyes saw my substance being yet unformed, and in your book they were all written, the days fashioned for me, when as yet there were none of them.*

A brief study of this passage thrills the mind. The word for *formed* in verse thirteen means to stand erect. God made man to stand upright, which implies that humans were not derived from an ape in an evolutionary process. To be "fearfully made" implies to be designed intricately. The Hebrew word means to be embroidered with a variety of color. Not only is the person intricately formed, he is indeed one of a kind with a unique DNA. God threw away the "cookie cutter" when he designed each human being individually. Remember that when David wrote Psalm 139, the sex of the fetus could not be determined as it can be today with modern technology. Only God could see the unformed babe in the womb. The meaning of the word for *frame* is that of power, and implies that someday this feeble, helpless fetus is going to become strong and grown up. God could picture that happening in the days and years to come, because He has a vested interest in His creation. What is the result of this creation? The psalmist marvels as the thought of the created human being brings wonder to the mind, and a confession that he realizes the greatest of God in that creation. Awe wells up in his mind and he gives glory to God. Indeed man is God's highest creation.

We now add another dimension to the creation of man. That is the recreation of the redeemed soul and the Church of Jesus Christ who give glory to God. Not only are we fearfully and wonderfully made, we are fearfully and wonderfully redeemed! We saw above that His sovereignty chose us, and His grace brought us to Himself. The response of our hearts is to sing for joy and bring glory to Him for what He has done. We examined this in the previous chapter as we looked at Ephesians 1:3-14. But as we look at the prayer of Paul in Ephesians 1:14-21, we see another dimension where the believers in Christ give God the glory. In Ephesians chapter one, Christ has placed us at his right hand positionally in heavenly places. Ultimately we will be with Him in reality when we enter heaven. In Ephesians chapter three, Paul attempts to have the readers comprehend the majesty of God in the mystery of calling His saints to Himself, and to know the love of Christ. How is this done? The more we grow in the grace and knowledge of the Lord, the better the Spirit of God helps us to grasp the wonder of our salvation.

But not only that. As the saints gather together and jointly exalt the Lord and study His Word together, that comprehension of the wonder of our salvation is expanded in the heart and mind of the believer. Remember, Paul is writing to the church of Ephesus, not just to individuals. Our salvation is a many faceted jewel which is revealed by the many saints who walk together with God. Paul hints at this when he talks about the variegated wisdom of God in Ephesians 3:10 made known by the Church.

The redeemed body of Christ is God's show piece for His glory. He holds her up as the example of His glory, taking a lost people and showing the world, especially the fallen world of principalities and powers, what He has done in displaying that power in creating the Bride of Christ. Only His wisdom could design such a glorious creation. Paul then concludes with these words in Ephesians 3:21, "To Him be glory in the Church by Christ Jesus to all generations for ever and ever, Amen." The Lord receives glory from us through His work in our lives. Is it any wonder that we are called to give glory and praise to Him in return for what he has done for us?

There are several passages in the Bible that can be used for benedictions. Examples of this include Numbers 6:24-26, Romans 8:31-39, especially the last two verses, 2 Corinthians 13:14, and Hebrews 13:20-21. But we close this section with Jude 24-25 because it refers to the glory of God, *Now to Him who is able to keep you from stumbling, and to present you faultless before the presence of His glory with exceeding joy, to God our Savior, Who alone is Wise, be glory and majesty, dominion and power, both now and forever Amen.*

The believer in Christ will stand before the glory of God. Can you imagine the circle of glory surrounding the person of God and His majestic throne? The marvel of grace allows the believer to do that, as he has no right of his own to stand before a holy God. But we read that God is keeping us for Himself so that we may experience that day. We cannot stumble out of His grace! And Satan certainly cannot take us out of God's hand. Only that which is holy can stand in the presence of Holiness. And that holiness is the righteousness of Christ indwelling us. The whole setting brings exceeding joy. Could this refer to the joy of the Father rather than the joy of the saints? God is so pleased to welcome us home that He is a picture of the father in the parable of the Prodigal Son in Luke 15. And this doxology in Jude ends with, "To God our Savior (and some manuscripts include "through Jesus Christ our Lord") be glory and majesty, dominion and power, both now and forever, Amen."

3. THE LORD JESUS CHRIST IS THE GLORY OF GOD

This subject alone could take a book of its own. The highest manifestation of the glory of God is found in the person and work of Jesus Christ. He is the perfect fulfillment of all that God designed in a human being, and the ultimate example of what it means to give glory to God. Hebrews 1:3 tells us that the Son is the brightness of God's glory as well as being the exact expression of God's image. The apostle John also bears this out when he records the prayer of Jesus in John 17:5. The Lord states that He shared the glory of the Father before His incarnation. But He retained that glory with the Father after He became man. Jesus is equal to the Father and therefore shares the Father's glory, whether it is before or after the incarnation.

The prophet Haggai makes an amazing comparison between the glory of the temple that Solomon built, which was destroyed by Babylon in 586 B.C. and the glory of the second temple constructed in Zerubbabel's time and completed in 515 BC. The second temple was not as beautiful nor majestic in sight as was the first one. But listen to what Haggai says of the second temple in Haggai 2:3,6-9, *Who is left among you who saw this temple (i.e. Solomon's temple) in its former glory? And how do you see it now (i.e. the rebuilt temple)? In comparison with it, is this not in your eyes as nothing? ...For thus says the Lord of Hosts: "Once more (it is a little while) I will shake the heavens and the earth, the sea and the dry land: and I will shake all nations, and they shall come to the Desire of All Nations, and I will fill this temple with glory, says the Lord of Hosts. The silver is Mine and the gold is Mine, says the Lord of Hosts. The glory of this latter temple shall be greater than the former, says the Lord of Hosts, and in this temple I will give peace, says the Lord of Hosts."*

There is a two-fold prophesy here. The prophet speaks of shaking the heavens and the earth. This probably refers to the end times when God will bring judgment on the earth.

But before that, God says that He will send the Desire of all Nations who will fill the temple with glory. Who is that Desire of Nations? It is none other than Jesus Christ who would come to earth several hundred years after Haggai's prophecy. The glory mentioned here did not come from man because the text says that God will fill the temple with <u>His</u> glory. It has nothing to do with earthly magnificence. God is pleased to fill the temple with the glory of Jesus' presence. It is another way for Him to say, "This is my beloved Son in whom I am well pleased." (Matt.3:17) When Jesus entered the temple in Jerusalem (i.e. Zerubbabel's temple which was renovated and expanded by Herod) to teach or worship, His glory was greater in the eyes of the Father than the magnificence of the glory of Solomon's temple.

When we think of the construction of a gorgeous temple, it may have walls or floors of gold or marble, majestic carvings of valuable gems, and intricate designs of enormous and lavish beauty. But these elaborate architectural designs are only the shell of the building, and do not fill the vacant area of the entire building. It is said of Solomon's temple that everything in it was overlaid with gold or had gold articles connected with it (1 Kings 7:50). But when Jesus came to the temple in Jerusalem, His presence filled the temple with the glory of God, and all the gold of the world could not exceed that glory of the Savior.

When we compare Haggai 2:3 with Ezra 3:12, it would appear that those who saw the first temple of Solomon wept when they saw the second which was not as magnificent as the first. They were sad that the glory of Israel as pictured in the first temple had departed when the second was constructed. But God had another thought, one which was to become the pattern for the New Testament age. The glory of Christ was to fill the temple of Jerusalem with His presence, and in God's eyes to become greater than the physical appearance of Solomon's beautiful structure. But after the resurrection of Christ and the formation of the Church of Jesus Christ, the glory of the temple which Jesus visited while on earth was to be transferred to the glory of the individual indwelt by the person of Christ. We are now the temple of God and a beautiful creation greater than the material structure of any earthly temple (2 Cor. 6:16; Eph. 2:20-22).

In what way is Jesus the Desire of All Nations? The Scripture says that He was "despised and rejected by men" (Is. 53:3). He came to His own creation and people and "His own did not receive Him" (John 1:11). However, to those whom God has called out from "every kindred, tongue, tribe, and nation", Jesus is the One whom men hunger for to find salvation (John 1:12).

If we go back to the time of Herod when Jesus was born, the world was ripe for the coming of a deliverer. In that sense the immediate prophesy of Haggai was fulfilled in His birth. As He lived among men, the people of His day sought Jesus for help with the hope that He would be the Deliverer of Israel from Roman authority and rule, misplaced as that desire was. His mission was greater than the immediate deliverance from a tyrannical dynasty on earth. It was to become the spiritual hope and peace of all humankind in His crucifixion and resurrection. God indeed has placed eternity in the heart of man (Eccl. 3:11) which will never be satisfied until Christ fills that heart with Himself. In truth, Jesus is indeed the Desire of all Nations!

We read in 2 Corinthians 4:6, "For it is God who commanded light to shine out of darkness, who has shone in our hearts to give the light of the knowledge of the glory of God in the face of Jesus Christ." This is an amazing compliment to the glory of God. People could see that glory when they saw the face of Christ as He walked on earth. We cannot be completely sure what that statement entails. It is safe to assume that Jesus did not have some heavenly halo or glow on His face. Scripture tells us that God's glory is so majestic that no man can look on Him and live (Ex. 33:20). But God's glory was evident in the life of Christ. That glory was veiled when He became a man. It was as though the human body of humility covered the glory of Christ. He never lost that glory, but it was not openly manifested during His lifetime except at the Mount of Transfiguration.

As we consider the story of the Transfiguration of Christ on the Mount, both Matthew and Mark describe the transformation that took place while Jesus was speaking with Moses and Elijah. In both passages Mathew 17:1-7 and Mark 9:2-8, the word used by both writers to describe the transformation of Jesus' appearance is the Greek word from which we get the English word *metamorphosis*. We do not know what that change in Jesus' appearance looked like. But the descriptions of Matthew and Mark suggest that His form was unlike that which ever happened in Jesus' life while He was on earth. Keep in mind that these Gospel writers were not on the mountain when this event happened. They may have gotten this account from Peter, James, and John who were there. Matthew's account of the transfiguration states that Jesus' face shone like the sun, and His clothes became white as light (Matt. 17:2). Mark declares that His clothes became as white as light and that there is no soap or detergent that could make them any whiter (Mark. 9:3). Although Luke does not use the word metamorphosis in his account of the story, he describes the incident in this way, "As He (Jesus) prayed, the appearance of His face was altered, and His robe became white and glistening" (Luke 9:29). With such a dramatic transformation as bright as the sun and as white as light, we can conclude that this was surely a display of His glory which was wrapped in humanity, but temporarily manifested on this occasion. Peter refers to this incident in 2 Peter 1:17 and states that the disciples who were present at this event, "were eyewitnesses of His majesty."

Another aspect of this truth can also be seen in the Gospel of John. In John 1:14, the incarnation is shown to be an example of the glory of God. John states that he, and others in his day, saw the glory of Christ as He walked on earth. This may also be a reference to the glory which Christ manifested on the Mount of Transfiguration. But he adds in the Johanan passage, "the glory as of the only begotten of the Father." The glory of the Father is expressed in the glory of His Son as he lived on earth. All of the gracious ways and truthful statements and teachings of the Lord expressed the glory of the Father as John and the other disciples saw these traits and teachings in the Son. Jesus was grace and truth incarnated. The Father also embodies these characteristics.

Some scholars believe that the Lord also manifested that effulgence of glory in the Garden of Gethsemane when He asked His captors whom they were seeking. When they answered "Jesus of Nazareth," the Lord said, "I Am (He)," and the soldiers fell backward (John 18:4-8). There is no Scriptural proof that Jesus did manifest His glory, but it is surmised by the action of the soldiers that Jesus' glory was indeed manifested.

In John 2:1-11 we read of the miracle that Jesus performed in changing the water into wine. We spend much time thinking about and studying that first miracle in Cana. Indeed that was miraculous and not to be minimized. However, in verse eleven, we are apt to overlook a phrase that is seminal in the life of Jesus. John states, "This beginning of signs Jesus did in Cana of Galilee, and manifested His glory" (John 2:11). His miracles were a manifestation of His divinity and thus of His glory which He shared with the Father.

In the resurrection of Lazarus, Jesus states that Martha and the other witnesses to Lazarus' revival would see the "glory of God" (John 11:40). That glory was miraculously displayed also when Jesus said to Lazarus "Come forth" (John 11:43). The conclusion is that the glory of the Son is synonymous with the glory of the Father. In both of these instances as in His other miracles, the purpose of Jesus was to give people a clear picture of the glory of God which indwelt Him.

In John 8:54 Jesus says, "It is my Father who glorifies me." We can go back to the baptism of Jesus as a context for the reason of this statement. In Mathew 3:17 we read of a voice from heaven saying, "This is my beloved Son in whom I am well pleased." In John 8:29, Jesus says, "I always do those things that please Him (the Father)." Again in John 17:4, Jesus says that He has glorified God on earth and completed everything the Father asked Him to do. Jesus performed miracles with the power indwelling Him. But this was also the power of the Father working through Him, and was a display of the Father's glory as well. Jesus lived every second of His life to the glory of the Father. Whatever Jesus did pleased His Father. In John 8:50, we read that Jesus never sought His own glory or attempted to vindicate Himself. Nor did He seek the praise of man, but always wanted to glorify the Father. Yet in not seeking His own glory, men glorified God and praised Him for the things that Jesus did.

In John 17:5, Jesus requests to be restored to the same honor which He had before the incarnation. His honor and glory was co-equal with that of the Father. He left that glory and honor to become a man. Philippians 2:8 refers to Jesus humbling Himself to become a man. In John seventeen He prays to be restored to that honor. But before that can happen, He will perform the greatest act in glorifying the Father in His incarnate state; He will die on the cross. Referring back to John 17:4, Jesus says that He has finished the work that the Father gave Him to do. This refers not only to His life, but His work on the cross. Jesus was viewing Calvary as an event that had been accomplished in His mind. We read of the agony in the Garden of Gethsemane, and of the cry of despair on the cross. For Jesus, this was already accomplished in His mind, as He was determined to carry out that act in the garden. Thus He could say that He has finished His work. With all of these references above we conclude with the truth that God's glory was evidently displayed in the person of Christ, and in His actions and miracles.

CHAPTER 11
THE GLORY OF GOD AMONG THE NATIONS

1. THE PROPHESY OF THAT GLORY

A key verse for the study of this topic is found in two places in the Old Testament with slight variation; Isaiah 11:9, and Habakkuk 2:14. The Habakkuk passage states, "For the earth will be filled with the knowledge of the glory of the Lord as the waters cover the sea." Both of these passages refer to the coming kingdom that will be set up on earth when the Lord returns. In Isaiah chapter 11, the context for this statement is couched in the coming of the Lord the first time with the Spirit of God upon His life (Is. 11:1-2). It continues with the circumstances in which He will reign at His second coming with righteousness and justice in dealing with the poor (V 4), judgment on the wicked (V 5), the change in the animal kingdom with creatures living together in harmony (V 6), and finally the Gentile world seeking the King (V 10). In the midst of this, the knowledge of the Lord, or the truth of His Word will spread among the peoples of earth. But Isaiah does not use the word glory in describing this scene. Habakkuk does. The Word of God and His glory are synonymous. As the Nations receive the Word and repent, the glory of the Lord is enhanced through the salvation of mankind.

Habakkuk deals with a different situation but the end result is the same. The nation of Judah is living in rebellion against God. Because of that God is going to send Babylon to punish Judah for these sins. The prophet has a hard time dealing with this. Babylon is even more wicked than Judah. How can God allow such a thing to happen? God answers Habakkuk's question by telling him that Babylon also will be destroyed. But beyond that, God will deal with the Nations of earth. The Lord says in Habakkuk 2:3 "The vision is for an appointed time", implying that the events He describes will happen to Babylon in the near future. God has His own inscrutable way of dealing with humankind. Habakkuk is to wait His timing for these events to unfold (V 3), and in the manner in which they will unfold. Some scholars believe that the phrase in verse three should be translated, "he will surely come", not "it will surely come," referring to the second coming of the Lord. This is the parallel to the Isaiah 11 passage. In His first coming, people are justified by faith (Habakkuk 2:4, cf. Rom. 1:17; Gal. 3:11, Heb. 10:38) in the One who is the Root of Jesse (Is. 11:1). When the Lord Jesus returns to earth again, (although that aspect of this prophesy is never mentioned in Habakkuk, but only implied), part of His dealing with the Nations at that time will be the knowledge of His glory that will cover the earth. Habakkuk does not understand the ways of God, but he concludes the prophesy in chapter 3:17-19 with a beautiful hymn of praise and trust in a wise God. ***Though the fig tree may not blossom, nor the fruit be on the vines; Though the labor of the olive may fail, and the fields yield no food; Though the flock may be cut off from the fold, and there be no herd in the stalls-Yet I will*** *rejoice in the Lord, I will joy in the God of My salvation. The Lord is my strength: He will make My feet like deer's feet, and He will make me walk on my high hills.* Habakkuk rejoices and gives glory to God for who He is, more than what the Lord provides for him in material goods. The word *rejoice* in the Hebrew language literally means to jump for joy The prophet is ecstatic at the way God is going to deal with His enemies in order to bring glory to Himself.

Another key verse regarding the glory of God is found in Psalm 8:9, "O Lord, our Lord, how excellent is your name in all the earth." The word *excellent* can also mean glorious. David is meditating on the works of God and especially the creation of man. Man is made a little lower than the angels, but still made in the image of God, and crowned with glory (Ps. 8:5). God has taken some of His glory and imparted that to man. But David's point is not about the glory of man. Indeed, he is only made a little lower than the angels. David's point is about the glory of God in general, since verse 9 is a repetition of verse 1. God's excellence and glory is framed in what He has done in making man, and is a prophesy of what God does as His normal operation.

Isaiah chapter 6 deals with the call of Isaiah and his vision of the holiness and glory of God. This is revealed to him personally. He hears the seraphim say in verse 3, "Holy, Holy, Holy is the Lord of Hosts, the whole earth is full of His glory." Commentators have suggested that the word *holy* being repeated three times is a statement of the holiness of the three persons of the Godhead. Father, Son, and Holy Spirit are all glorious in holiness. The seraphim saw this from eternity past, and are shouting the same thing in Isaiah's day. In his commentary, Delitzsch says of Isaiah 6:3, "The design of all the work of God is that His holiness should become universally manifest, or, what is the same thing, that His glory should become the fullness of the whole earth." (Keil & Delitzsch Vol.7 1983, 193). This adoration of God and His glory will continue throughout eternity.

To further enhance this truth, the apostle John quotes extensively from Isaiah 6 in John 12:40-41, *He (God) has blinded their eyes and hardened their hearts, lest they should see with their eyes, lest they should understand with their hearts and turn, so that I should heal them." These things Isaiah said when he saw His glory and spoke of Him.* In the context of John chapter 12, the apostle is talking about the Savior. The Isaiah passage quotes the seraphim referring to the person of God. The apostle Paul also makes reference to the Isaiah passage in Acts 28:26-27 while he was imprisoned in Rome awaiting his trial. There he is speaking to the Jews about the person of Christ and the salvation of the Jewish nation. All three texts, Isaiah chapter 6, John chapter 12, and Acts chapter 28 refer to the rejection of the Jews both to the message of God and the rejection of the Messiah. By this rejection the Jews also rejected the glory of God that was manifested to them in the Old Testament.

A similar passage with the same truth is found in Numbers 14:21, "But truly as I live, all the earth shall be filled with the glory of the Lord." The context of this verse has a very vital truth connected to it with the Isaiah passage. In both places, the theme is the rejection of Israel to the ways of God, and a rejection of His glory over that nation. Israel is complaining against Moses after the spies return from scouting the land of Canaan. The people believe the report of the 10 men who said that it was fool hearty to go into the land and attack giants. Joshua and Caleb think differently and attempt to plead their case for advancing and attacking the Canaanites. But the people reject that argument. In response, God wants to destroy the Israelites for their lack of faith. Moses intercedes for the people and asks God to forgive them. It is at this point that the words of Numbers 14: 21 are spoken by the Lord. God in His mercy does spare the people but is deeply offended because the Israelites have forgotten the multiple indications of God's presence and glory in His leading the children of Israel out of the land of Egypt, and sustaining them in the wilderness to this point in their journey.

God declares that His glory will be seen over all the earth. Surely the immediate truth of this verse would be fulfilled when the Canaanites see the marvelous way that God defeats them and drives them from the land. But "all the earth" is much greater than Canaan. God will eventually declare His glory to all humankind. This verse in Numbers can also be taken as a prophesy of the coming of Christ who will declare the glory of God, and to whom a waiting world would hear that message from God's servants. In reality, God wanted the Israelites to tell of His glory to all the nations of earth (Ps. 96:3; 98:2). But they failed, even as Isaiah and Paul stated. But the truth of this statement by the Lord will be completely fulfilled when the Lord Jesus returns in glory, and all nations, and particularly Israel, see that glory.

2. THE GOSPEL AS A REVELATION OF GOD'S GLORY

There are only two verses in the New Testament which state that the Gospel is glorious. One is found in 2 Corinthians 4:4, "...Lest the light of the Gospel of the glory of Christ, who is the image of God, should shine on them" (that is on the unsaved). The other passage is 1 Timothy: 1:11, "According to the glorious Gospel of the blessed God which was committed to my trust." Both passages are written by Paul. However, there are illustrations which show how the glory of God was manifested in the Gospel. That revelation is given to those to whom the Gospel was hidden or purposely rejected. 2 Corinthians 4:4 tells us that Satan is the culprit behind the rejection of the Gospel. A person may reject the message, but Satan has a part in his unbelief and rejection. God has to perform an unusual work in the heart of the person or people to show that His work of salvation is glorious. It is interesting that the apostle Paul, formerly known as Saul, uses that phrase, since he of all people was shown the glory of God when he met the Lord on the Road to Damascus.

His road to Damascus experience is the most dramatic conversion in Scripture. On his way to persecute Christians, Saul is confronted with a blinding light that stops him dead in his criminal tracks. Along with the light, the voice of the Son of God is used to reveal Jesus to the apostle. Saul is a dedicated Jew who honestly believes that he is doing God a favor by persecuting the believers (1 Tim. 1:13). He vehemently believes that Jesus is blaspheming when He declares Himself to be the Son of God and God Himself. Those who espoused this doctrine of Christ's Deity in Saul's day were worthy of death. It takes God's glory to intercept him in his wicked plans. Saul is completely baffled, both by the light and the voice. He cries out, "Who are You Lord" (Acts 9:5)? When Jesus reveals Himself, Saul's immediate response is, "What do you want me to do?" The power of the Gospel is so great that the unbeliever's response is one of submission. He is temporarily blinded physically, but his blind mind is now opened to the glorious Gospel.

The "Gospel of the glory of Christ" and the "glorious Gospel" in the two passages mentioned above basically mean the same. In what way is the Gospel glorious? From the story of Saul, we see the glorious display of God's majesty, along with a glorious plan of salvation to a sinner and the glorious effects that accompany the plan. The brightness of God's glory is contrasted with the blindness that falls upon Saul before he is brought into the marvelous light of understanding the truth of the Gospel. The principle that we glean from this is that no matter how dark the blindness set forth by Satan, the light of God's glory in redemption will always overcome that darkness. That is what makes the Gospel so glorious!

But we see another truth from the glorious Gospel. It is the transformation of people by the Gospel that is so glorious. Second Corinthians 4:4 states, "But we all, with unveiled face, beholding as in a mirror the glory of the Lord, are being transformed into the same image from glory to glory, just as by the Spirit of the Lord." There are three phenomenal words in this passage that help us to understand the glory of Christ revealed in the Gospel. The first is the word *unveiled* (*anakalupto*). In context, Paul is referring to the veil that Moses wore over his face when he came from the presence of the Lord to talk to the people (Ex. 34:25). His face shined with the glory of the Lord, and the people could not look at him unless he covered his face with a veil. Paul is saying here that the veil of the blinded mind of the unbeliever has been uncovered by the Gospel to enable the person to comprehend the glory and majesty of the message.

The next word to note in this verse is *beholding* (*katoptrizo*). The word in the original Greek should be translated, "beholding for oneself in a mirror." The divine glory of the Gospel is unveiled, as it were in a mirror, and we look into the mirror to see that glory. As Moses beheld the Lord's glory which was reflected in his face, so also we behold the Lord's glory in the Gospel, and that glory is reflected in our lives. But in contrast to Moses, we do not have to look on the glory of the Gospel with a veiled face. We can see it openly as God reveals Himself to us. We are privileged to behold all of the character of God in His beauty and perfections as a believer in Christ through the mirror of God's Holy Word. That is mind boggling! But that is not all!

There is a third word to observe; *transformed* (*metamorphosis*). We saw this same word above in conjunction with the Lord's transformation on the Mount of Transfiguration. Our lives are changed into the same image by that which we behold in the mirror of the Gospel. Paul is using a cultural metaphor to describe this affect. The commentator Barnes in his notes has this thoughtful remark concerning 2 Corinthians 3:18, *It is possible that there may be an allusion here to the effect which was produced by looking into an ancient mirror. Such mirrors were made of burnished metal, and the reflection from them would be intense. If a strong light were thrown on them, the rays would be cast by reflection on the face of him who looked on the mirror, and it would be strongly illuminated. And the idea may be, that the glory of God, the splendor of the divine perfections, was thrown on the gospel, so to speak like a bright light on a polished mirror; and that that glory was reflected from the gospel on him who contemplated it, so that he appeared to be transformed into the same image. (Barnes Vol. 11 1962, 131)*

The image of God's glory placed in Adam, was lost in the fall. He was the glory of God in his creation. Now in Christ Jesus, that glory is restored through the glorious Gospel that God reveals in changed lives. This is for everyone, not just for the one person or nation, as was the case in Israel, when only Moses saw that glory.

3. THE GLORY THAT IS YET TO COME

We have made some preliminary observations of that glory in the prophesies of Isaiah 11:9 and Habakkuk 2:14. No one knows the exact day or date of the fulfillment of these prophesies, but from Scripture we know that it is coming. Our thesis is that the glory of God is the magnificence of all things, and is revealed in many ways. We can also conclude that this event is inevitable. The prelude to that glorious event is mentioned in a couple of passages in the New Testament. Philippians 2: 9-11 describes the day in which all mankind, both saved and unsaved will bow the knee to King Jesus and acknowledge Him to be Lord, ***Therefore God has highly exalted Him and given Him a name which is above every name, that at the name of Jesus every knee should bow, of those in heaven, and of those on earth, and of those under the earth, and that every tongue should confess that Jesus Christ is Lord, to the glory of God the Father.*** The context of this verse also suggests that along with humankind, the entire angelic world of both saved and lost angels will someday acknowledge the Lordship of Jesus Christ. In His exalted position as Redeemer King, the Son stands alone as worthy of praise from the lips of all creation. The glory which He willingly laid aside temporarily when He was on earth some day will be restored to Him. This concept should also be studied in conjunction with Ephesians 1:20-23.

In 1 Corinthians chapter fifteen, we read that all saints who died will be raised again to life when the Lord Jesus returns from heaven. Those living at the return of Christ will be changed and taken to heaven along with the resurrected saints. The Father sovereignly ordains men to eternal life and gives those believers to the Son who become His possession, and part of His bride, the Church. At the end of the age, the Son returns those redeemed ones back to the Father in honor so that the Father may be eternally glorified in the redemption of His elect (1 Cor. 15:28). The Father will be declared sole Ruler of the universe. This glorious scene ties in beautifully with Jesus' priestly prayer in John 17: 2, 5 and shows the intimacy and unity of relationship between Father and Son, *As You (Father) have given Him (Son) authority over all flesh, that He should give eternal life to as many as You have given Him...And now, O Father, glorify Me together with Yourself with the glory which I had with You before the world was. (parentheses mine).*

We turn next to the book of Revelation for a further description of that exultation. The word glory is mentioned 16 times in the book of Revelation. We read of those who ascribe glory to God. In Revelation 1:6, the apostle John gives glory to the Lord Jesus Christ for His work of redemption. The four living creatures and the twenty four elders who stand encircling the throne of God give glory to the Father in Revelation 4:9,11 for His creation. A similar picture is painted in chapter 5:9-10 where both living creatures and elders give praise to Jesus Christ for His salvation. However, the text says that the twenty four elders wear crowns and cast them at the foot of the throne, while ascribing worthiness to Christ. The living beings apparently do not have crowns. It would seem that the twenty four elders are human beings who have been redeemed, possibly representing the twelve tribes from the Old Testament and the twelve apostles from the New Testament. The four living beings are angelic in form. This is consistent with Revelation 5:11 which states that tens of thousands of angels (literally myriads of myriads or thousands of thousands) sing the song of redemption. What do angels know about being saved from sin and hell? Experientially they do not fit with humankind in praising the Lord Jesus for His work on the cross and the resurrection. But they join in harmony with those who have experienced this salvation.

In a broader picture, the work of Christ redeems all creation both animate and inanimate, which would include the angelic hosts of heaven. The crescendo of glory to God continues to build. We started with the living beings and elders who are joined by a gigantic chorus of angels Now in Revelation 5:13-14, we read, *And every creature which is in heaven and on earth and under the earth and such as are in the sea, and all that are in them, I heard saying: "blessing, and honor, and glory and power be to Him who sits on the throne, and to the Lamb forever and ever!" Then the four living creatures said, "Amen." And the elders fell down and worshipped.*

This scene is too awesome for words. Any and every created thing that has the breathe of life gives glory to both Father and Son. No one is omitted in this chorus of praise which would include the underworld demons. Can you imagine the majesty and glory of this event if this happens in one huge oration or oratorio? Again in Revelation 5:12, the angels speak, as do all creation in 5:13-14. But in Revelation 5:9 the living beings and twenty four elders sing a new song (literally ode) because the refrain contains the concept of redemption by the blood of Christ. The divine chorus master, whoever that person is, will create a song that has never been sung until that time, which specifically is written for the theme of redemption.

In Revelation 7:9-12, we read of a great multitude from every tribe, people, and nation who shout the theme of salvation which they have experienced. Following that, we see again the angels, living beings, and twenty four elders giving glory to God. However, in Revelation 11:13, the scene shifts with unsaved people on earth giving glory to God after an earthquake. People were in awe of the power of God. Tragically they do not repent of their sin. They would only recognize that God was the One who performed this act. But in Revelation 19:1, the same shout of praise and glory rises to God for salvation which He has ordained.

These are the expressions of those who give God the glory that He rightfully deserves. But His own glory also lights the heavenly city of Jerusalem in Revelation 21:11, 23. There is no need of the sun or moon in a place where God dwells in inexpressible light. This light is not like an ordinary light that we see from the sun. Scripture tells us that the light has the aura of a jasper stone. Jasper is an opaque quartz which may be red, yellow, or brown in color. The closest object that we can equate with this type of light might be the northern lights with their waves of brilliant color filling the sky. Anyone who has seen the northern lights stands in rapt attention and awe at the sight of its beauty. Perhaps this is what the light of God's glory looks like in heaven.

We conclude that everything in this creation points to the ultimate end of our existence, which is to give God the praise and worth due to Him because of who He is and what He has done for us. Worshipping the Lord can be considered as the highest form of giving Him glory!

CHAPTER 12
MISSIONS AND GOD'S UNFOLDING
PLAN OF REDEMPTION

We are indeed richer Christians in understanding the way God deals with us in sovereignty, grace, and glory. But if we only want to learn more of this truth, and do not make an application in putting these truths into action in our lives, we have missed the purpose of the book. What is that purpose? It can be summed up in one statement: His redeemed elect are left on earth to tell the story of His sovereignty, grace, and glory to an unsaved world. It is the story of missions! We can and should revel in what God has done for us. But that is insufficient. We have been commissioned to tell this story, and have others revel with us in what God has done in their lives. John Stott summarizes it succinctly with the following statement, *We engage in evangelism today not because we want to, or because we choose to, or because we like to, but because we have been told to. The Church is under orders. The risen Lord has commanded us to go and preach, to make disciples, and that is enough for us. (Stott 1967, 37)*

Dr. Marvin Newell sets forth that responsibility for the believer to share the message of Christ. In his excellent book *Commissioned*, Marv makes a careful examination of the five so called "Great Commission" passages, and delineates the emphasis that Jesus makes in each charge. Newell then presents what he calls *The Great Commission Diamond* consisting of the messenger, message, the strategy to evangelize, disciple, and to plant churches. The goal of this model is world evangelism (Newell 2010, 93-110). Just as a diamond has many facets, so there are any number of ways to carry out the Great Commission. But one thing is certain; it must be carried out by those of us who have been saved. That is our obligation. Methods and strategies may change but the message is always the same. God is in the saving business of recovering lives from sin's tragic results, and He wants believers to tell that story to a lost world. The approach suggested in Newell's book is but one way to tell that story. It begins with God, is carried out by God, and ends with God. It's all about Him!

1. MISSIONS AND SOVEREIGNTY

In chapter two, we considered God's sovereignty in relation to individual salvation. We now want to focus on His sovereignty as it relates to a lost and dying world. We want to put the Great Commission in context to God's role in the calling of lost men. There are any number of verses in the Bible from which we could choose a passage that touches on this theme. Malachi 1:11 states, ***For from the rising of the sun, even to it's going down, My name shall be great among the Gentiles; In every place incense shall be offered to My name, and a pure offering; For My name shall be great among the nations, says the Lord of Hosts.***

The context of this verse is very interesting in light of verse 11. The Jewish priests who were the spiritual leaders of the children of Israel were dishonoring the name of the

Lord by offering imperfect animals as sacrifices to God This action greatly offended the Lord. In verse ten, God says that He has no pleasure in their offerings and will not accept them. But He goes on to say that His name will be honored among the Gentiles. Malachi mentions that incense will be offered in every place, not only in the temple. This implies that God looks beyond the physical temple of worship where Jewish sacrifices and incense were performed. The prophet predicts that Gentiles will offer their sacrifices wherever the Gospel is spread to see the name of the Lord exalted everywhere. A new and more glorious sacrifice, the death of Christ, will bring men to worship God and offer the incense of their prayers throughout the pagan world. The entire Old Testament sacrificial system will be exchanged for the work of the cross and the resurrection.

Notice two things from this verse: God's name will be great. This may refer to His glory among the Nations. Secondly, His name will be spread among all the Nations. The same Hebrew word is used twice for nations or Gentiles. God is emphasizing the extent to which He wants to spread the truth of salvation.

The book of revelation is clear that people from every tribe and nation will be represented in heaven. (Rev. 5:9; 7:9). But as we look around the world today, we see that God in His sovereignty has chosen more from one nation than another, just as He has chosen one individual over another. The same question must be asked and still remains unanswered, "Why has God chosen some and not others?" Jesus died for a lost world, and shed His blood for all mankind, including every tribe, tongue, and nation. But the same answer must be given to that question as was given above: we cannot discern the sovereign mind of God, but we must be involved in getting out the Gospel message according to the Great Commission. The work of redeeming and transforming lives among the Nations is God's sole responsibility. As redeemed children of God, we have the privilege of taking part in executing God's plan of bringing people to Himself. But be sure of this; God will raise up others to reach the lost world if we as individuals neglect our personal responsibility to heed His calling to go and preach the gospel. The work is God's and His methodology is mainly the sending of men and women to bring this good news to a lost world. Either we take up this challenge personally, or God will raise up people in our place to do so.

We can truly rejoice today in the effectual calling of God to people from every nation. God is using His witnesses around the world, as well as extraordinary methods such as dreams, visions, and miracles to call to salvation those whom He has chosen. But there is a common denominator that completes the transaction of salvation in the lives of the unsaved, and that is the presence of the Word of God. 1 Peter 1:23-25 reminds us that, ***Having been born again, not of corruptible seed, but incorruptible through the Word of God which lives and abides forever, because "all flesh is as grass, and all the glory of man as the flower of the grass. The grass withers, and its flower falls away, but the Word of the Lord endures forever."***

Romans 10:17 also emphasizes this truth, "Faith comes by hearing, and hearing by the Word of God." Whether or not God uses the preaching of man or extraordinary means, the person or people will come to Him through the revelation and enlightenment of the Word of God in the heart.

In his excellent article posted on the Internet entitled *The Sovereignty of God and the Christian Mission,* Rev. John Samson has summarized succinctly the relationship of the sovereignty of God and the calling of mankind. He states,

1. Missions exists to display the utter and paradoxical sovereignty of God.
2. Missions is empowered by the utter paradoxical sovereignty of God.
3. Missions is advanced through a paradoxical victory in defeat, which demonstrates the utter sovereignty of God.

God's sovereignty is revealed not only as the means of salvation, but as a perfect display of the character of God. As believers go to the ends of the earth, the power of God takes weak believers and paradoxically uses them to powerfully work in bringing dead men to life in Christ. Some witnesses are tortured and killed for the sake of Christ. But this shows unsaved people the worth of the Gospel and the length believers are willing to go to die for it. Again, we are reminded that this study of the sovereignty of God and missions is to be put into practice. We are responsible as believers to be involved with God and a lost world. May we join God in HIS sovereign program to reach the Nations of the world.

2. MISSIONS AND GRACE

Since God is sovereign and has foreordained who will be elected to salvation, and since that salvation process is all of grace apart from what man can do, why should the church of Jesus Christ be involved in reaching a lost world? This is an age old question. When William Carey began his quest to reach the unsaved, he was advised by church leaders that if God wants to save the world, He can do it apart from man going to tell the story of the Gospel. John Calvin had the best response to that seeming dilemma. He said that he did not know whom God had chosen for salvation. It was not his responsibility to know, but it was his responsibility to go and preach the Gospel so that men might hear the call of God and allow God to do the choosing. Calvin was correct! We do not have the capacity to look into the heart of God or into the hearts of men and know whom God has chosen as His children. The Scriptures give several reasons why we must be involved with preaching the Gospel of grace to a lost world;

1. The primary motive is to enhance the glory of God through the bringing of souls into right relationship with Him (Ps. 96:3).
2. The commission of Christ calls us to tell others (Matt. 28:19-20). We are ambassadors or representatives for Christ (2 Cor. 5:20).
3. The love of Christ is in our hearts, and He gives us a sense of gratitude to desire sharing the message (2 Cor. 5:14; Eph. 2:4). We should be overwhelmed so greatly by what God has done in saving us that we want to share that news with others.
4. Our concern for others (John 1:35-41; 4:29; 5:15; 9:27).
5. The sense of God's call to share the Gospel is urgent. God has placed the burden and responsibility on our hearts to tell others (Rom. 10:14-15; 1 Cor. 9:16; 9:20). Paul was called by God and believed that he had an obligation to fulfill that calling. It is the same with us.

6. The imminent return of Christ compels us to share the message (1 Cor. 15:51-52; 1 Thess. 4:13-18). When the Lord returns, the lost will be left behind to suffer tribulation, and possible eternal loss of the soul (2 Thess. 1:7).

7. The judgment of God is coming on unbelievers (2 Cor. 5:11). Paul was burdened that God would bring condemnation on the unsaved, and he wanted to deliver them from this judgment.

That is exactly why this key doctrine of the grace of God is tied in so beautifully with missions. God has commissioned us to go, and we have no choice but to obey that command if we are to be obedient children of God. Not only that, we are also reminded that His using redeemed believers is His chosen method to bring men to Himself. He would not have commissioned us to go if He did not intend to bring men to Himself through our participation. Can He save men apart from believers proclaiming the message? Certainly, because He is all powerful to do so. But He chooses not to function that way.

But what is this grace? From the context of the Titus 2:11-12 passage cited above, it seems that it refers to the appearing of Jesus Christ, who is "Full of grace and truth" (John 1:14). We saw that Jesus was gracious and He embodied the concept of grace in salvation, pardon from sin, and the on-going results of a life changed by grace. He was grace personified. But some also believe that the Titus passage refers to the message and teaching of grace as a doctrine to be conveyed to lost souls. Both of these concepts may be true. Jesus Christ is God's unmerited favor sent to a lost world. The Lord is the Person and the message that we proclaim to that lost world that will change men to live godly lives as seen in Titus 2:12. This Person and message has appeared to all men.

Philip is an excellent example of the message of grace in Acts 8:26-40. God prompts the Ethiopian eunuch to read the Word of God which the Lord knows will bring enlightenment for salvation to the eunuch. But God also tells Philip to go along the desert road to meet the traveler and explain the plan of grace and salvation, leading to the eunuch's conversion and baptism. It is God Who orchestrates the conversion from start to finish. He has chosen the eunuch for salvation, and when the moment of that salvation draws near, God sends an unknown messenger with an unknown destiny to go along an unknown path to meet an unknown man. He alerts Philip to see the man reading a Scripture roll of Isaiah chapter 53. With the Lord's prompting to speak to the man, the evangelist inquires of the eunuch's understanding of that reading. The spiritually hungry Ethiopian asks Philip to help him understand the reading, and this results in the eunuch's conversation.

Grace is the modus operandi that God uses to bring men to Himself. Titus 2:11 states "The grace of God that brings salvation has appeared <u>to all men</u>" (underline mine). Notice the universality of that statement. All men (women and children included) everywhere are exposed to the grace of God. That is His way in reaching the world with the Gospel. In Paul's day the word grace (*charis*) was normally used in conjunction with a relationship to a friend. Paul uses this word in conjunction with a lost world that has rebelled against God. We are His enemies, but He has extended His grace. That tells us the heart of God is really bent on desiring the salvation of all, even though the concepts of election and foreordination to salvation must be included in the equation of this mystery. That is the reason grace is wrapped up with the concept of missions.

We may think of Paul as the ultimate example of the apostle of grace and missions. This can be clearly seen in his statement in 2 Corinthians 5:18-6:1. The extended passage is quoted in its entirety because of the manner in which he so eloquently calls men to salvation. *Now all things are of God, Who has reconciled us to Himself through Jesus Christ, and has given us the ministry of reconciliation, that is, that God was in Christ reconciling the world to Himself, not imputing their trespasses to them, and has committed to us the word of reconciliation. Now then, we are ambassadors for Christ, as though God were pleading through us: we implore you on Christ's behalf, be reconciled to God. For He made Him who knew no sin to be sin for us, that we might become the righteousness of God in Him. We then as workers together also plead with you not to receive the grace of God in vein.*

Paul has been redeemed by God and as Christ's ambassador he has been commissioned to preach the Gospel of reconciliation to lost men. What is his plea? Do not ignore the grace of God. Grace is tied directly with the heart of a missionary cry for men to be saved, and redeemed Man is directly tied with God in the proclamation of that message. Paul uses the phrase "workers together" to indicate this truth. The message of reconciliation is the message of grace. Note his statement of God's exceeding abundant grace that saved him in 1 Timothy 1:12-14. Paul urges lost men not to reject the grace of God.

But we have a problem. If a saved person has been chosen and predestined for salvation, how can that person refuse to receive the irresistible grace of God? What is Paul saying here? He is saying that as Christ's ambassadors, he is preaching the gracious offer of reconciliation to a lost world. Some people will reject God's offer of grace, and some will receive it. The Lord freely offers His grace to all people, but those not chosen will reject that grace. Yet they are responsible for rejecting the offer of grace, salvation, and reconciliation. The theme of missions can never be separated from the offer of grace that God so richly extends to a lost world. And we must be involved in that message of grace as part of our Great Commission responsibility.

3. MISSIONS AND THE GLORY OF GOD

We began the study of this topic on the glory of God by saying that the sole purpose of our lives is for God's glory and His eternal satisfaction. The Puritan scholar Jonathan Edwards stated that in order to realize how glorious God is, we need to come to the point of proclaiming His glory to the Nations. What could bring God more joy and satisfaction to our lives than to see multitudes of people from every nation, tribe, and language gather around His throne and sing His praises for all eternity? Indeed, that is what is happening every day of the year as multitudes are confessing Christ as Savior. What additionally could bring God more pleasure than seeing His children proclaim that message of His glory to a lost world? We are in harmony with God when we fulfill His purposes to bring Him glory. One way of doing this is to tell the story of salvation. The story of missions is the story of the glory of God to redeem the world.

The Old Testament emphasizes the theme of missions and God's glory. Before Solomon built the temple the Jews worshipped in the Tabernacle. David built the Ark of the Covenant and placed it in the tabernacle. After placing the

Ark, David sings a song of thanksgiving in 1 Chronicles chapter 16. Among his praises are the following words, ***Sing to the Lord all the earth; proclaim the good news of His salvation from day to day. Declare His glory among the nations, His wonders among all peoples...Give to the Lord, O families of the peoples, Give to the Lord glory and strength. Give to the Lord the glory due His name; Bring an offering and come before Him. Oh, worship the Lord in the beauty of holiness. (1 Chron. 16:23-24; 28-29)***

Not only was Israel to give God glory, but they were to proclaim that glory to the Nations? Why? Because the Nations had idols that could not save them. Only Jehovah could redeem, and the Israelites were to make that message known to the heathen world.

Again in Psalm 72:19 David writes, "Blessed be His glorious name forever! And let the whole earth be filled with His glory, Amen and Amen." God has always had a missionary heart, and throughout all generations He has desired that the message of His glory be transmitted through His children. Unfortunately, Israel, the main communicator with God at that period of time, failed to carry out His wishes.

In Revelation 21:24, 26 there is a reference to the kings of the earth bringing their glory and honor into the holy city of Jerusalem. This would be in conjunction with the honor that they have received as redeemed leaders. The kings bring that honor and glory to the Lord.

In Revelation 16:9 we read that the unsaved refuse to give glory to God as He pours out His wrath on their unbelief. The text says that the unsaved blasphemed God. The conclusion is that humankind who will not give glory to God and repent of their sin will suffer judgment. The Creator and Redeemer of the universe is worthy of all glory from His creation, and those who fail to acknowledge that glory suffer the penalty for their lack of adoration. Revelation 5:9, and 14:3 tell us of the blessing to those who do give glory to God, ***And they sang a new song, saying: You are worthy to take the scroll, and to open its seals; for You were slain, and have redeemed us to God by Your blood out of every tribe and tongue and people and nation, and have made us kings and priests to our God: and we shall reign on the earth.... They sang as it were a new song before the throne, before the four living creatures, and the elders, and no one could learn that song except the hundred and forty four thousand who were redeemed from the earth.***

God receives glory from the angels, as well as from His creation (Ps. 19:1). But He delights especially to receive glory from those whom He has redeemed. The Brooklyn Tabernacle Choir so eloquently expresses this truth with their song which says, "But the greatest song of all is the song of the redeemed." Humans were His highest creation. But sin ruined them. Now that God has redeemed His chosen ones, His highest prize is for His children to glorify Him, and to incorporate them into the Church of Christ, which is His body. In Revelation 14:3 the 144,000 redeemed saints confess their salvation before the throne of God and the living creatures and elders. Can you imagine the testimony of these saved ones telling of their condemnation under God's wrath and judgment, only to be delivered by the blood of Christ and the grace of God? It will be a new song. We do not know what this means or what the new song is. Certainly we who have been saved can now sing a new song to our God. Isaiah 42:10 enjoins us to sing a new song to the Savior. Will this song in heaven be a greater and more glorious melody that the Lord Himself has composed for us to sing around His throne? If so, how utterly awesome that song will be!

But let us expand this thought a little further! God created humans for His glory. When Adam and Eve sinned, that glorious image in them was marred, but not completely destroyed or removed from them. God was and is jealous for His name and wants to restore that glory in His creation, but not at the expense of His own character. In the book *The One Year Walk With God Devotional*, Chris Tiegreen suggests that God hates sin so much, that He was willing to allow His glory in the creation of humanity to be laid aside rather than to allow sin to prevail. Tiegreen says, ***His passion and zeal throughout Scripture to make His name known among the peoples of the earth was subverted by His own hand. Why? He hates sin. It cannot stand. It would have been a greater offense to God for Him to defend a rebellious people for His name's sake than to let the symbol of His name fall into the hands of pagan enemies. So He did the latter. The glory of God was held captive for our sin. (Tiegreen 2004, 267).***

In God's plan of missions, we see the method that God used to restore both humankind and God's glory in His creation of man. That method is seen in the redemption of humanity and the creation of Christ's Bride, the Church. Going back to the opening thoughts in the book from Ephesians chapter one, we are told that we are to the "praise of His glory." There we looked at the thoughts from a theological basis. Now we are examining the thoughts from an outreach basis. In Ephesians 3:9-10 we read of the mystery and wisdom of God, ***To make all see what is the fellowship of the mystery, which from the beginning of the ages has been hidden in God Who created all things through Jesus Christ, to the intent that now the manifold wisdom of God might be made***

known by the Church to the principalities and powers in the heavenly places.

In Colossians 1:26-27, we read of the glory of this mystery, **The mystery which has been hidden from ages and generations, but now has been revealed to His saints. To them God willed to make known what are the riches of the glory of this mystery among the Gentiles which is Christ in you, the hope of glory.**

The glory of this mystery is the glory of missions: the body of Christ created in redemption and indwelt by the person of Jesus Christ and the indwelling Holy Spirit. What greater glory could God orchestrate for His own pleasure than to create a Bride for His beloved Son composed of both Jews and Gentiles? That is all inclusive, because it contains people from every tribe, kindred, tongue, and nation. But there is something even more beautiful about this thought. From these verses in Colossians, we see the sovereignty of God (God willed), the grace of God in bringing men and women to Himself in salvation (Christ in you) , and the glory of God in fulfilling His purpose in man through His new creation. Every time we evangelize a person or a people group, we are fulfilling the desire of the heart of God.

We close with one final thought. The ultimate expression of the glory of God related to missions is found in Philippians 2:9-11, **Therefore God also has highly exalted Him, and given Him the name that is above every name, that at the name of Jesus every knee should bow, of those in heaven, and of those on earth, and of those under the earth, and that every tongue should confess that Jesus Christ is Lord to the <u>glory of God the Father</u> (emphasis is mine).**

For the believer and the Church, there is praise to God's glory for the redemption the Body of Christ has experienced. For the unbeliever, there is a confession of praise to God even though he has rejected the offer of grace and salvation through Christ. Those "under the earth:" expressing praise may refer to the unredeemed dead, or to demons. In any case, all these categories of people will relate to God's glory based on their personal salvific relationship to God. That is because they will acknowledge the name of Jesus Christ as Lord and that name brings honor to God's glory. In stating that Jesus is Lord, the people acknowledge His sovereign rule and ownership over their lives. They are saying that God's glory, and not their own is the focus of living. In brief, it is story of missions that determines the joy or sorrow of expressing praise to God's glory through Christ. I challenge every reader to see the beauty of God's character as it relates to His burden for a lost world, and to be involved with His heart of redemption as best and as much as possible while we have the privilege and opportunity to do so.

QUESTIONS FOR DISCUSSION

CHAPTER 1

1. How has the title of this book affected your view of God and salvation?
2. In pondering the question "Why am I here" what conclusion(s) have you come to as to the reason for your existence?
3. Recall an incident in which you have seen the sovereignty of God intervene in your life.
4. From the concepts presented in chapter one, what is your understanding of the steps in becoming a child of God?

CHAPTER 2

1. What key word does Paul use in the opening verse of His doxology?
2. Distinguish between the two types of blessings mentioned in the chapter. Which one is emphasized in both Old and New Testaments?
3. What do you think "in the heavenlies" refers to?
4. State what you think is the foundational blessing in salvation?
5. What does Kenneth Wuest suggest to be the purpose for which God has chosen us? Are you fulfilling that purpose?
6. Describe the relationship between God's calling, and man's response to that call?
7. Describe how Paul shows every aspect of God's plan of salvation to be His sovereign work.

CHAPTER 3

1. Do you ever question God's dealings in your life? How have you resolved those questions?
2. How do you respond when you know that God can do anything He wants with your life, and you are helpless in your circumstances
3. How has God created people in His image? How should this affect day to day living?
4. Describe in your own words what it means to have Adam's sinful nature.
5. Describe the way in which God delivered man from his sinful condition.
6. Can you relate an event in your life in relation to your salvation which clearly showed that God was involved with that event?

CHAPTER 4

1. From the incidents described in this chapter, what is your opinion of God's dealings with the United States?
2. Can you add to the stories related in this chapter on the sovereign intervention of God in the course of human events?
3. Share a story from your own experience relating to God's sovereignty or providence in your own life.
4. Go back to the Old Testament and search for scriptures that show God's sovereignty over the nation of Israel, and His attitude toward those who despise Israel.

CHAPTER 5

1. What additional verses can you find that tell us to pray?
2. What are the conditions for God's forgiveness for our sins when we pray?
3. Do you believe that prayer changes things? Explain your answer.
4. Is God obligated to answer the believer's prayers? The unbeliever's prayers?
5. How does our praying bring pleasure to God?

CHAPTER 6

1. Define the word grace in your own words.
2. Describe an instance in which you believe that God was especially gracious to you.
3. What synonyms can you suggest for the word grace?
4. In addition to the examples given in the book, give another illustration from both the Old and New Testament of the gracious dealing of God with humankind.
5. What word(s) would describe the truth that the way of salvation is the same in both Testaments
6. In your own words, describe how the righteousness of Christ has become your righteousness before a holy God.

CHAPTER 7

1. What is the relationship between sovereignty and grace?
2. What are the effects in a life when grace is the modus operandi in sanctification?
3. What do you think is the believer's position under grace in relation to the Ten Commandments?

4. Discuss the manner in which legalism defeats the believer in his Christian life?
5. State the attitude of God toward the believer when he sins and then confesses that sin?
6. What do we mean by the term "cheap grace?"

CHAPTER 8

1. Describe a time when you have seen the grace of God manifested in another person's life.
2. What is your reaction to the concept of choosing pain over comfort for the sake of experiencing God's grace in your life?
3. Explain the expression "future grace." How does this apply in daily life?
4. How did David and Joseph show grace in their lives in relation to their antagonists?
5. How do we claim the grace of God in dying?
6. Describe how the grace of God is synonymous with the Holy Spirit in the life of the believer?

CHAPTER 9

1. How would you define the concept of the glory of God?
2. Describe how you think God jealously guards His glory.
3. Explain in your own words how every aspect of God's character enhances His glory.
4. What do we mean by the thought that we cannot increase the glory of God?
5. In what way(s) does God reveal His glory through the Church?Are you included in that glory? Why do you believe this?

6. State the two aspects of election that enhance the glory of God.

CHAPTER 10

1. Give an example of both good and fallen angels who give glory to God.
2. Describe an occurrence in nature that showed the glory of God to you.
3. In God's mind, what is the highest illustration of His glory being displayed?
4. How have you seen the Church enhance the glory of God in your life?
5. Compare the magnificence of the temple in Haggai chapter two, with the temple in Jerusalem in Jesus' day. What makes the one better than the other?
6. What has replaced the glory of the temple in Jerusalem and the presence of Jesus preaching in that temple?
7. In what way was Jesus' miracles a display of God's glory in Him?

CHAPTER 11

1. Distinguish the difference between the expressions found in Isaiah 11:9, and Habakkuk 2:14 What is the common thread that ties them together even though the expressions are different?
2. Give examples of people in Scripture who saw the glory of God, and describe the context in which they witnessed the glory.
3. When Israel sins in rejecting God, what is she actually doing?
4. What stopped Paul in his tracks on the way to Damascus?

5. What passage states that all creation everywhere will bow to acknowledge the glory of Christ?

6. In your opinion, which book of the Bible best describes the glory of God?

7. What do you think is the highest form of glory that we can give to God?

CHAPTER 12

1. Summarize Newell's Diamond Strategy of evangelism. What aspect of the Diamond best fits your gifts and calling?

2. In addition to the Word of God, what other method(s) is God using today to reveal Himself to an unsaved world?

3. Which of the several reasons or motives for evangelism most prompts you to share your faith with another person?

4. Can you share an experience of a conversation you may have had with an unsaved person that is similar in nature to Philip's unusual experience with the Ethiopian eunuch?

5. If you have led a person to Christ, relate that experience to others for their encouragement.

6. Explain in your own words the manner in which God's glory is held captive by our sin. What aspect of His glory was held captive?

7. How is the Bride of Christ enhanced?

BIBLIOGRAPHY

Ames, Dr. William. *Sanctification*. On line sermon notes, n.d.

Barnes, Albert. *Barnes Notes*: 14 Vol. Grand Rapids: Kregel Pub., 1962.

Berkhof, Louis. *Systematic Theology.* Grand Rapids: Eerdmans Pub. Co., 1949.

Boice, James M. *God's Providence*. On line publication, n.d.

Breuer, William . *Unexplained Mysteries of World War II*. Edison, NJ: Castle Books, 1997.

Bruce, F.F. *The Gospel of John*. Grand Rapids: Eerdman Pub., 1983.

Brown, Colin. Gen. Ed. *The New International Dictionary of New Testament Theology: 3 Vol.* Grand Rapids: Zondervan, 1981.

Butler, Trent C. Gen. Ed. *Holman Bible Dictionary*. Nashville: Holman Bible Pub., 1991.

Chafer, Lewis Sperry. *The Epistle to the Ephesians*. Grand Rapids: Kregel Pub., 1991.

Chapell, Bryan. *Holiness By Grace*. Wheaton: Crossway Books, 2001.

Childers, Thomas. *World War II: A Military and Social History.* Chantilly, VA: The Teaching Company, 1998.

Gill, John. *John Gill's Exposition of the Entire Bible.* E-Sword. Electronic Bible Study. www. e-sword.net, 2005.

Han, Nathan E. *A Parsing Guide to the Greek New Testament.* Scottdale, PA: Herald Press, 1971.

Hendryx, John W. *The Sovereignty of God and World Missions*. Internet. n.d.

Hendriksen, William. *Ephesians*. Grand Rapids: Baker Book House, 1967.

Henry, Matthew. *Commentary In One Volume*. Grand Rapids: Zondervan Pub., 1961

Hodge, Charles. *Romans*. Wheaton: Crossway Books, 1993.

_____. *Systematic Theology: 3 Vol*. Grand Rapids: Eerdmans Pub., 1979

House, H Wayne. *Charts of Christian Theology and Doctrine*. Grand Rapids: Zondervan Pub. House, 1992.

Jamison, Robert, A. R. Faucett, & David Brown. *Commentary on the Whole Bible*. Grand Rapids: Zondervan Pub. House, 1962.

Keil, C.F. & F. Delitzsch. *Commentary on the Old Testament: 10 Vol*. Grand Rapids: Eerdmans Pub., 1983.

Kittel, Gerhard. Ed. *Theological Dictionary of the New Testament: 10 Vol*. Grand Rapids: Eerdmans Pub. Co., 1972.

Kohlenberger, John R. III Ed. *The Expanded Vines Expository of Dictionary of New Testament Words*. Minneapolis: Bethany House Pub., 1984.

Little, Christopher R. *The Revelation of God Among the Unevangelized*. Pasadena: William Carey Pub., 2000.

Longman III, Temper & David E. Garland. *Gen Eds. The Expositor's Bible Commentary: Ephesians-Philemon Vol. 12*. Grand Rapids: Zondervan Pub., 2006.

Massey, Rev. Jerry. *Sermon: The Christian Grace of Forgiveness*. Internet; n.d.

MacArthur, John. *The Sovereignty of God in Salvation.* Sermon notes; n.d.

Meyers, Rick. *E-Sword.* Electronic Bible Study. www.e-sword.net; 2005.

Murray, John. *Redemption Accomplished and Applied.* Grand Rapids: Eerdmans Pub. Co., 1961.

Newell, Marvin J. Commissioned: *What Jesus Wants You To Know As You Go.* Wheaton: Church Smart Pub., 2010.

Orr, James Ed.. *International Standard Bible Encyclopedia: 5 Vol.* Grand Rapids: Eerdmans Pub., 1930.

Packer, J.I. *Evangelism and the Sovereignty of God.* Downer's Grove, IL: Inter-Varsity Press, 1961.

Pink, A.W. *The Sovereignty of God.* Carlisle, PA: Banner of Truth Trust, 1996.

Paton, Jeff. *The Grace of God: Part 6, A Theology of Sin.* Internet Study; Oct. 3, 2011.

Piper, John. *Desiring God. Sermon: The Pleasure of God in All That He Does.* Internet; Feb. 1, 1987.

_____. Desiring God. *Sermon: The Glory of God.* Internet; Oct. 12, 1976.

_____. *Future Grace.* Sisters, OR: Multnomah Books, 1995. Reisinger, John G. Sanctification by Grace. On line sermon, n.d.

Ryle, J. C. *Expository Thoughts On The Gospels: 4 Vol.* Grand Rapids: Baker Book House, 2007.

Samson, Rev. John. *The Sovereignty of God and the Christian Mission.* Internet; n.d.

Snipes, Eddie. *Living in Grace.* www.exchangedlife.com, On line sermon, 2013.

Stewart, Chris & Ted Stewart. *Seven Miracles That Saved America.* Crawfordsville, IN: Shadow Mountain Press, 2009.

Storms, Sam & Justin Taylor Eds. *For the Fame of God's Name: Essays in Honor of John Piper.* Wheaton: Crossway Books, 2010.

Stott, John R. *One Race, One Gospel, One Task: Vol. 1.* Minneapolis: World Wide Pub., 1967.

Strong, James. *Strong's Exhaustive Concordance of the Bible.* Nashville: Abingdon Press, 1980.

Thayer, Joseph Henry. *The New Thayer's Lexicon of the New Testament.* Peabody, MA: Hendrickson Pub., 1981.

Tiegreen, Chris. *The One Year Walk With God Devotional.* Wheaton: Tyndale House Pub., 2004.

Thussen, Peter J. *Predestination.* New York: Oxford University Press, 2009.

Unger, Merrill F. *Unger's Bible Handbook.* Chicago: Moody Press, 1967.

Vincent, Marvin R. *Word Studies in the New Testament: 4 Vols.* Peabody, MA: Hendrickson Pub., 2009.

Walvoord, John F. *The Revelation of Jesus Christ.* Chicago: Moody Press; 1966.

Walvood, John F. & Roy B. Zuck. Eds. *The Bible Knowledge Commentary.* Wheaton: SP Pub., 1985.

Ware, Bruce. *For the Fame of God's Name: Essays in Honor of John Piper.* Wheaton: Crossway Books, 2010.

Webster's II *New Riverside University Dictionary.* Boston: Houghton Mifflin Co., 1984.

Wiersbe, Warren. *Classic Sermons on the Sovereignty of God.* Grand Rapids: Kregel Publications, 1994.

Wigram, George V. & Ralph W. Winter. Eds. *The Word Study Concordance.* Pasadena: William Carey Pub., 1978.

Wikipedia. *Dunkirk Evacuation.* Internet, n.d.

Wuest, Kenneth. *Word Studies in the Greek New Testament: Ephesians.* Grand Rapids: Eerdmans Pub. Co., 1953.

_____. *The Pastoral Epistles in the Greek New Testament for the English Reader.* Grand Rapids: Eerdmans Pub. Co., 1960.